1⁰⁰   2.00
10-16

Best Herbs

Stefan Buczacki
Best Herbs

HAMLYN

Executive Art Editor Mark Richardson
Designer Michael Whitehead
Editor Selina Higgins
Production Melanie Frantz
Picture Research Jenny Faithfull

First published in Great Britain in 1995
by Hamlyn an imprint of Reed Consumer Books Limited
Michelin House, 81 Fulham Road, London SW3 6RB
and Auckland, Melbourne, Singapore and Toronto

Produced by Imprimerie Pollina SA n° 66792
Printed in France

ISBN 0 600 58338 4

A catalogue of this book is available at the British Library

CONTENTS

INTRODUCTION · WHAT IS A HERB?

It's an interesting word, herb, with different meanings for different people. And as I have described some plants that might be thought surprising inclusions in a herb book, while just possibly having omitted one or two that might have been expected, you are entitled to an explanation.

Calendula officinalis, **an excellent culinary and ornamental herb**

To a botanist, the word herb is short-hand for the term herbaceous plant, which is one that differs from a tree or a shrub in lacking any woody frame-work and more or less dies down in the autumn to survive the winter as a rootstock. But clearly that definition won't suffice for present purposes as there are several shrubs and some trees in the book. As the name derives from Latin, through French, do those languages help us? Not much, for *herba* in Latin means grass or more or less any green plant while to a French speaker, *une herbe* is simply a plant, or again, more specifically grass, while it is often modified in such terms as *herbe marine* (seaweed) or *mauvaise herbe* (weed).

The first recorded use of 'herb' in English specifically to mean a plant that has some culinary or medicinal value was in 1290 and subsequently Chaucer used it too but even today, it is employed with varying scope. Thyme is generally recognised as a kitchen herb, but what about parsley; sage is generally perceived as a herb but what about onion? And where do lettuce and celery fit in; or apple and blackcurrant? Where do vegetables and fruit end and herbs begin? I don't know, and so I've devised my own def-initions and, as far as culinary use is concerned, I've included only those plants that are used principally to add specific flavours to dishes and meals without being major edible compo-nents in their own right. So parsley and some types of onion are in; but lettuce and apple are out.

Not all herbs, however, are culi-nary; indeed some are poisonous but are used, or have been used in the past, for medicinal purposes. I have included a large number of species that fall into this category. By and large, however, I have left out those plants whose only use has been as a source of dyes for this is a large, rather complex and specialized sub-ject that is of interest only to a very small number of gardeners. I have also generally excluded plants that qualify solely for what I may best call house-hold uses such as pan scouring, pest control or even pot-pourri, for which it seems almost every scented plant under the sun has been used at one time or another. Which brings me to

my final point. This is a gardening book, not a cookery book or a medi-cinal herbal. I have written it from the standpoint of a gardener who wants to grow a range of herbs to use in the kitchen but who also has an interest in those many others with medicinal roles, without necessarily being likely ever to want to try them. So while I have indicated the general kitchen uses, I have given no recipes. And even more importantly, I have given no details of the way that herb plants are prepared for medicinal use and must emphasize that this is not some-thing to be undertaken without expert guidance and knowledge.

So, I hope you will grow a large number of herbs in your garden, will find many of them attractive in their own right, will enjoy using some in your cooking and will find much inter-est in familiarizing yourself with those that have, over the years, performed intriguing and sometimes remarkable medicinal roles.

An example of a mixed herb garden, showing the attractive combination of variegated and flowering herbs

SITE AND SOIL

Herbs are rather more demanding in respect of their soil and site requirements than many of the plants that you will grow in your garden. Although there are some notable exceptions, it's fair to say that most grow best in light, fairly free-draining, alkaline and not very rich soils; and in full sun. Of course, not all gardeners have these conditions but because herb gardens are generally fairly small, it is usually possible to amend the existing soil to bring it closer to the optimum, even if this means creating a small raised bed in which to do it. There is little that can be done if your garden beds are all shady, although even there, it may be feasible to grow some herbs in containers on a sunny patio or path edge, as I've described on p.18.

Before you can begin to amend your soil, you really need to understand how different soils vary and how many changes can and cannot be made. All soils are made up of differing amounts of clay, silt, sand and humus. (Stones and pebbles don't play a part in this although a soil with plenty of pebbles in it is no bad thing for herb growing as the pebbles will usefully help to retain heat.) A soil that contains a high proportion of clay will be slow to warm up in spring but then stays warm and will also contain a good supply of nutrients. In dry conditions, however, clay soils will become hard and impenetrable whereas in the wet winter weather, they may become waterlogged; precisely the wrong conditions for herbs. By contrast, a light, sandy soil will warm up quickly, cool down quickly and, being free-draining, lose both water and nutrients rapidly. Humus, which is simply part-decomposed organic matter, will improve both types of soil because it contains natural gel-like substances that bind together soil particles to form crumbs and also help the retention of moisture by their sponge-like properties. For this reason, you should always dig in compost, manure or other organic matter before planting in order to ensure moist, fertile soil.

I've mentioned that many herbs require at least slightly alkaline conditions, but, to be more precise, they require a pH of above 7. The pH scale is a measure that runs from 0 to 14, and whereas soils with a pH above 7 are alkaline, those with a pH below 7 are called acid. Most soils lie naturally somewhere between about pH 6 and pH 7.5 (and are more or less neutral, therefore) and most herbs will be happy in these kinds of conditions but distinctly unhappy if the soil is appreciably acid, that is below a pH of about 5.0. The pH of a slightly acid soil can be raised fairly simply, however, by adding lime, and this procedure is well worth doing in the autumn before planting up a new herb garden in the following spring.

Ruta, Thymus and *Tanacetum* all like a warm site and a well drained soil

DESIGN AND STYLES OF HERB GARDENS

I often find myself saying to gardeners that only if they really insist will I give them ideas and suggestions for the way their gardens should be designed and planned. This is nothing to do with avoiding the issue, or trying to save myself some work. It is simply that a garden is such a personal creation that I feel the best results are achieved when people design them for them-selves, perhaps with some profes-sional pointers over practical pitfalls. So, by this token, you can plant up a herb garden exactly as you wish and no-one, least of all me, will criticise you for it. But there is another dimension to growing herbs and it's one that I allude to on p.6 where I stress that this is a gardening book, not a cookery book or a herbal.

A mixed potager-style planting of herbs and vegetables

Much of the interest in herb growing is an historical rather than a practical one, and much of early gardening was carried out for herbal reasons. Many of the methods of planting herbs that were developed over the years were extremely attractive and many people are drawn to the idea of a herb garden that mimics in some way these very traditional growing methods. Such a planting can fit very happily into an otherwise modern garden.

But before outlining how an histori-cally inspired herb garden can be planned, let's just start with a very simple planting of herbs for someone who does, indeed, only want a small collection of herbs for use in the kitchen. It should not need saying (but in my experience, it often does), that

they should be planted as close to the kitchen as possible, commensurate with the requirements for sun and soil (p.8). It really is surprising how a few more metres to walk will deter busy cooks from making full use of the fresh herbs that are available. To grow what I would consider a basic range of herbs for the kitchen (see my list on p.11) you will need an area of about 2 x 2m (7 x 7ft); ideally 3 x 3m (10 x 10ft). Remember to plant the taller types at the back and then, most importantly, put in some stepping stones, for a herb garden is unlike an ornamental flower bed in that you will need to walk in and among the plants as you snip and collect. Without stepping stones, you will find you have a compacted soil and muddy shoes –

another inconvenience if you have just stepped out while in the middle of stirring a sauce. And that is all there is to it: easy to plant, easy to maintain.

And so now to the historically inspired herb garden and, be it medieval or Victorian in its inspira-tion, the watchword is formality. The design will be based on angles and symmetry. Measure accurately the area that you have available for plant-ing and transfer the outline to scale on squared paper; this is one of the very few instances in garden planning where I find it necessary to plan a planting with this degree of precision. Allowing for the smallest individual planting unit or bed of about 60 x 60cm (24 x 24in), examine ways in which the whole can attractively be

DESIGN AND STYLES OF HERB GARDENS

Herbs need not be confined to the back of a house; here brilliant thyme borders line the path to the front door

divided up. Bear in mind always the need for access to all parts, even if not to pick and collect herbs, then for maintenance. Paths dividing up the discrete parts of the area could be of grass (fiddly to mow in confined space and also giving you a great deal of edge trimming), bricks (arranged in any number of patterns; time-consuming to do but visually superb although you must use durable types that won't crumble); or gravel (easy, cheap, very attractive but annoying and messy if you have to walk over it with muddy boots). Mortared pebbles and stone slabs are less effective as they are less

formal; concrete or other modern slabs or blocks will look frightful unless they are very good copies of brick paviors.

If you have room and want a mediaeval or Tudor feel to the planting, then use edging plants around the beds. The best by far is the compact and common form of box, *Buxus sempervirens* 'Suffruticosa' (see p.114) although *Santolina* (p.95) and other plants are sometimes used as cheaper, short-term substitutes. If you are really ambitious, then the box could be planted in knot garden fashion, the miniature hedges imitating the pattern

of knotted ropes. In a design of this complexity, you must mark on your squared paper the precise position of each of the edging plants. Then with canes and string, mark out the actual area to be planted and, square by square, plant up the herb garden, following the marked positions on your design very carefully.

I don't know who first planted up herbs in the gaps between the spokes of a wooden cartwheel laid on the ground, but it is an idea that caught on and certainly is a very simple way of creating an attractive, formal planting in a small area. If you can't obtain a

Basic Herbs for the Kitchen

Allium sativum Garlic

Allium schoenoprasum Chives

Anthriscus cerefolium Chervil

Artemisia dracunculus French
tarragon

Foeniculum vulgare 'Purpureum'
Bronze fennel

Helichrysum italicum Curry plant

Laurus nobilis Sweet bay

Mentha suaveolens Apple mint

Melissa officinalis 'Aurea'
Variegated Lemon balm

Ocimum basilicum Sweet basil

Origanum vulgare 'Aureum'
Golden oregano

Petroselenum crispum 'Moss
Curled' parsley

Rosmarinus officinalis 'Miss Jessup's
Upright' Rosemary

Salvia officinalis Sage

Thymus vulgaris 'Silver Posie'
Variegated thyme

Herbs flourish when planted in easily accessible beds set in paving

real cartwheel, then the pattern can be laid out, in whatever size you prefer, in bricks. But this, again, is just a suggestion and I return to my notion that gardens are personal and you should create and plant yours however you wish. Look at the designs in old gardening books (even ancient works have been reprinted in recent years) for your inspiration and think, also, of perhaps creating a themed garden – of aromatic herbs, of the herbs mentioned by Shakespeare, of plants used to control fevers, of white-flowered herbs, of Chinese herbs; but above all, have fun with plants that are, by and large, easy to grow and steeped in historical and mythical interest.

The lavender surrounding this path will give off a heady scent

PLANTS AND PLANTING

There are two main ways of buying new herb plants: by shopping personally at your local garden centre, or by obtaining them from a specialist herb nursery, which is likely to have a much wider range and to supply the plants by mail-order. At a garden centre, the plants will be in small pots; mail-order plants these days may well be dispatched in small plastic modules, packed together in sophisticated and very ingenious packaging which ensures they can be sent safely and reliably. Although herb plants in containers may, in theory, be planted at all times of the year, they are, in general, much less robust than shrubs or herbaceous border perennials and so are best bought and planted in spring or autumn, the periods when mail-order suppliers tend to send out their stock.

As I explain on p.14, most herbs, especially the shrubby types, aren't long-term plants. But this shouldn't mean that their planting positions are prepared any less thoroughly than long-lived plants. They are generally fairly small, however, and for this reason, it's easier to prepare and plant up a sizeable patch of the herb bed at a time, than to try the much more fiddly operation of making a precise planting position for each individual.

I find it worthwhile to double dig a herb bed in advance of planting, or at least to dig in compost (generally better than animal manures for herbs) to a good spade's depth.

Once you obtain your plants, from whatever source, and do plant them promptly so that they are able to establish without delay. The planting position should be prepared by digging a hole of approximately twice the volume of the pot ball of compost or about four times the volume if the plant is in a mailing module. The soil removed should be mixed with a roughly equal volume of compost or similar organic matter and a handful of bone meal. This is rich in phosphate, which aids root development and will help the plant to establish quickly. In addition, I always tease away the roots lightly around the edge of the compost ball as otherwise they tend to grow inwards, towards the more moist compost in the centre rather than out into the surrounding soil. Once the plant is in its planting hole firm the soil carefully with your boot or, if it is a small plant, with the handle of your trowel as you fill the hole, but don't ram it down too hard. Ensure that you finish by making a small mound with the soil sloping away from the plant's stem. This will prevent water from collecting at the base, and then freezing and causing damage. Finally, remember to water the plant well after planting.

FOOD AND WATER

Food and water are, of course, important for all garden plants although, as a group, herbs probably require less than many others. They are not generally grown for large and lush flowers or fruit which would necessitate a high level of potash. And although for the majority, it is the leaves that are

Basil seedlings ready to be pricked out

harvested and used, too much nitrogen, which is generally advocated for leafy growth, can also be detrimental. High nitrogen feeds are fine for leafy plants like cabbages that grow relatively quickly, but with smaller-leaved and generally slower-growing herbs, it can result in soft, watery and rather tasteless foliage. In general, therefore, I would recommend a light dressing of a balanced general feed containing roughly equal percentages of nitrogen, phosphate and potash. I find that fish, blood and bone, containing a nitrogen (N), phosphate (P) and potassium (K) ratio of around 5:5:6, serves the purpose admirably.

Water is important, too, and the herb garden, with its sunny position and free-draining soil can often be a dry one. I recommend applying a light organic mulch once or twice each year at times when the soil is damp. Almost any of the normal organic mulching materials can be used but, because herbs are usually small plants, the grosser materials like very coarse compost are best avoided and I tend to use fine compost or, best of all, well-rotted leaf mould.

Herbs can be propagated easily by seed; trays of seedlings can be moved outdoors to harden-off

AFTER-CARE AND PROPAGATION

By and large, herbs aren't plants to be left undisturbed for long periods. Most of the herbaceous perennials soon become too large for their allotted space and most of the small shrubby types become leggy and unkempt after two or three years and require replacing. There are also a few annual and biennial species that are obviously the most short-lived of all. So regular renewal of the plants is an important part of herb growing and while one option is simply to buy anew from your garden centre or nursery, it is much cheaper and very much more satisfying to propagate your own from your existing stock; provided the plants are healthy. Propagating from diseased plants will merely perpetuate any problems.

There are three main ways in which herbs may be propagated: from seed, by division, and by cuttings. I'll deal with each in turn. Most types of herb can be raised from seed; but many types, certainly of culinary herb, shouldn't. This is simply because the best varieties do not come true from seed and so must be propagated vegetatively, by division or cuttings. Nonetheless, many medicinal herbs and, of course, the annuals and biennials among the kitchen types can and should be raised from seed and this may be done very easily. Seed can be sown either outdoors, in the final growing positions, or in a greenhouse or other protected place from which the plants must be hardened-off before being planted out.

INDOORS

To sow seeds on the greenhouse bench or the kitchen window ledge, be sure to buy them fresh, packeted and branded from a reputable supplier. You will require a compost in which to sow them, a propagator, water, in most instances light and some means of supplying an adequate temperature. The compost should be a proprietary mixture, either soil-based or soilless but always use fresh for each batch of seeds.

There are many types of propagator and at its simplest, these need be no more than a plant pot. In practice, small plant pots are ideal for herbs as you won't need many plants of each type. Several small pots can be stood inside a standard-size plastic seed tray covered with a purpose-made rigid plastic cover with adjustable vents. These are usually purchased complete with the seed tray base and the same device can also be used for striking cuttings. But whatever equipment you adopt, ensure that it is disinfected and washed before being used again.

Generally, seeds require a slightly higher temperature in order to germinate than the plants will ever require again. Moreover, within fairly well

Dipping a sage cutting in hormone rooting powder before striking

defined limits for each type of seed, the higher the temperature the more rapid and uniform the germination. Provision of an adequate and appropriate temperature is thus extremely important, but remember that it is the temperature of the compost, not the air above it, that really matters (what gardeners call 'bottom heat') and the best way to provide this is with a purpose-made sand bench containing an electric heating cable or a heating mat, on which the propagators are stood. Some models operate at low voltage so a wire may safely be run to the greenhouse from the house if you

have no independent greenhouse electricity supply. Thermostatic control should enable you to regulate the heat fairly precisely but do pay careful attention to the temperature recommendations given on the seed packet.

Once the seedlings are showing their green cotyledons (seed leaves) above the compost, open the vents on your propagator half-way. As the seedlings stand upright and elongate, the vents should be opened fully and when the first true leaves have expanded, the cover should then be removed. It's always very important to attend to watering carefully at this

stage and to ensure that the seedlings are not exposed to direct hot sun. Sow two or three seeds to each pot, pull out the weaker seedlings if more than one emerges, and there will then be no need to prick them on. But you do need to harden them off.

The place to harden-off seedlings is the cold-frame, into which the pots of seedlings are placed. I always allow at least two weeks for hardening-off before planting out. In the first week, the frame cover is left half open in the day-time but closed up at night. In the second week, it is left fully open in the daytime and half open at night. If you do not have a cold-frame, the pots of seedlings may be put outside in the daytime and taken under cover at night, although this is laborious, and an inexpensive cold-frame makes a very worthwhile investment.

OUTDOORS

Gardeners talk of obtaining a good tilth before sowing seeds. Tilth is a curious, almost indefinable quality that I can perhaps best sum up as the soil condition in which seeds will germinate and seedlings will grow most satisfactorily. This means, in practice, that the soil crumbs must be broken down finely enough for the tiny roots to be able to make fairly unimpeded progress while, at the same time, there must be enough pores between the crumbs to ensure that the roots are well furnished with water and air. The soil must also be uniform in its structure, and all of these attributes combine to ensure that it warms up evenly and quickly.

The sowing area should generally be roughly dug, and organic matter incorporated in the autumn, then left with

Placing cuttings in rooting medium using a small wooden dibber

AFTER-CARE AND PROPAGATION

Covering the cuttings with a plastic dome to retain moisture

and discrete areas within the herb garden should be prepared for them, the soil being carefully raked away for sowing and then raked back again afterwards and carefully firmed. But always sow sparingly and, if necessary, thin out the seedlings to the spacing recommended on the packet if too many emerge.

DIVISION

Division is the simplest method of multiplication. This may be an old gardening adage but it is a true one – large clumps of herbaceous perennials can be pulled apart and the smaller pieces replanted. The best times of year to do this are autumn or early spring and the procedure is straightforward enough. Dig up the mature clump with a fork and pull it first into two, then more pieces. If possible, do this by hand, but if not, by inserting two forks, back to back, and levering them apart. Never use a spade as this is very likely to sever and damage the roots. From a clump of about 15cm (6in) diameter, it should be possible to obtain approximately 10 new plants but always tear off and discard those parts that lay in the centre of the original crown, as these will degenerate and never give rise to any vigorous new growth.

CUTTINGS

There are three main types of cutting: softwood, semi-ripe and hardwood. The names are self-explanatory and reflect the time in the season when each should be taken – softwood early on in the growing cycle, and hardwood at the end. Although it is hardly ever essential, hormone rooting powder may be used with all types but it is most beneficial with softwood types.

fairly large clods to overwinter. By the spring, the winter rains and frost will have broken these down but the soil will still be in a lumpy and uneven state, and there will certainly be some weed growth. The soil should then be dug again, using fork rather than spade, the weeds removed and the large lumps broken down with the back of the fork. This operation can be performed as soon as the soil begins to dry out in the spring – the precise timing will obviously vary with the part of the country in which you live and with the nature of your soil; as

I mentioned on p.8, a sandy soil will be in a workable condition much sooner than a clay one. About one week before sowing, the area should be raked to remove any remaining large clods and, at the same time, a balanced general fertilizer should be scattered over the soil and thus incorporated into the first upper few centimetres. Rake alternately in directions at 90° to each other in order to obtain as level a surface as possible.

On the whole, herb seeds are best broadcast sown; that is, scattered in small groups rather than straight lines,

Vigorous herbs, such as mint, can be contained by planting them in pots which are then sunk in the bed

With the exception of hardwood cuttings, all types should be rooted (or 'struck') in a covered chamber, either a propagator of the type used for seed sowing, or a covered cold-frame. It is very important to maintain a moist atmosphere around the cuttings for they will otherwise lose water through their leaves at a time when, lacking roots, they are unable to replace it from below. Even with a covered propagator, therefore, you should pay careful attention to the moisture content of the rooting medium and use a hand sprayer to mist over the cuttings regularly. The cold-frame can also be used for hardwood cuttings, although I prefer to root these in a sheltered spot in the garden, inserting the shoots in a narrow 'V'-shaped trench in the bottom of which I have sprinkled a layer of sand. The type of medium (sand, soil-based compost and so forth) into which the cuttings are placed varies with the type of plant and my suggestions are in the individual descriptions.

In general, cuttings should be removed from the parent plant with a clean cut made just below a bud. Evergreen shrubby herbs, such as sweet bay, can present problems for even if cuttings are taken during their dormant season in the conventional hardwood manner, the presence of leaves means that water will still be lost at a time when the plant has no means of replacing it. The difficulty can often be overcome by layering – the process where a stem is anchored into the soil while it is still attached to the parent plant. The disadvantage is that some patience is needed, as layerings rarely root satisfactorily in less than 18 months.

HERBS IN CONTAINERS

It should come as no surprise that herbs can be grown in containers, for most types of plant can. The advantage of growing them in this way is that, even people with very tiny gardens can have a small collection of useful herbs on a paved area or path edge. Also, an even smaller collection can be maintained on an indoor windowsill in a flat or in the house during winter when outdoor plants have died down.

I always use a soil-based compost (John Innes No.2 is ideal) and I always use ornamental terracotta pots, partly because they look so appropriate, but also because they allow the compost to breathe and are much less likely to encourage the root rotting that can happen so easily in plastic pots. Do be sure that the containers have adequate drainage holes and don't allow them to stand in saucers of water. Plenty of water and free drainage are essential for successful herb growing.

Choose a pot of appropriate size to the vigour of each type of plant (I have given details of plant sizes in the individual descriptions), and do keep one pot for each type of herb. Although a mixed planting of different herbs might look attractive initially, their varying growth rates will soon make for problems.

The only pot sold specifically for herb use is the so-called parsley pot, a tall pot with holes in the side through which the plants emerge.

Many herbs trail attractively

Herbs grown in containers can act as an extension to the herb bed

Potted sage and mint

Well planted, they look extremely attractive but there is a trick to planting them. If you completely fill the pot with compost and then try to push in the plants through the holes, you will damage the roots and they will be unlikely to establish satisfactorily. The secret is to put in compost only up to the level of the first holes and then carefully push the plants through the holes from the inside, then add more compost up to the next holes and so on until the pot is full.

Do experiment with your container growing; plant some herbs in hanging baskets and window boxes (pot them up individually within the window box so any that fade or require replacing may readily be replaced), and group together containers of different sizes. Always be sure to position containers in a warm and sunny position, don't neglect watering during the summer and be prepared, especially with large and vigorous plants, to give a little extra feed in the form of a balanced liquid fertilizer once or twice during the growing season.

There are a few rather special uses of containers that I mention in the individual descriptions of each herb. These are for those very vigorous plants, such as mint, that would otherwise, and very quickly, take over an entire herb garden. As I have suggested on p.22-4, the solution is to grow herbs like this in containers and to then sink the entire container to rim level in the soil.

Garden mint potted up for winter

A mixture of herbs with upright and trailing habits filling a window box

Wall-mounted planters for herbs

PICKING AND PRESERVING HERBS

The best way to use herbs is to pick them fresh from the garden. Just as with vegetables and salads, this is the great advantage of growing your own rather than relying on the shop-bought product. But even with the seasonal extension you can achieve by growing small herbs indoors in pots, it just isn't possible to have everything fresh all year round. For medicinal use, moreover, some type of preparation is almost always necessary. As I have explained earlier, however, this is a gardening, not a cookery or medicinal book and I shall make no attempt to venture into the intricate details of using herbs for either purpose, but I hope that the following guidelines for picking and preserving culinary herbs especially, based on my own experience, will be helpful.

Always take care not to eat or preserve herbs that have been sprayed with any chemical and, however they are to be treated, those for preserving should always be picked fresh. Dried or frozen herbs are never as good as lush, fresh herbs; but even dried or frozen herbs are better than brown or yellow herbs. The leaves of annual or deciduous types should be picked while they are young, which will generally mean in the early part of summer. They may be picked from evergreen species at any time of the year, although the fresh new leaves are always preferable. It's generally thought that leaves are best picked in the early morning before the heat of the day causes their volatile chemical components to evaporate and dilute.

Flowers are best picked just before they open fully, and fruits and seeds when they are fully ripe, but before they fall or are shed. This will probably mean watching and testing them over a period of a couple of weeks, cutting off the seedheads carefully, tying bags over them and then hanging them up in a warm but well ventilated place to complete the drying process.

Although the traditional way of preserving herbs is to dry them, there is no denying that the flavour is considerably inferior to that of the fresh product; dried parsley, for example, is about as tasty as dirty sawdust. For those herbs for which it does remain the best or only method, I now always use the microwave oven for drying even though some herbalists claim that the more subtle flavours and properties are lost. Freezing is an excellent technique for preserving herbs of most kinds; certainly delicate types, such as parsley, really do freeze admirably. There is so little to the operation that there is absolutely no excuse for not freezing some of your favourite summer herbs for winter use when very little is available fresh from the garden: simply put the herbs in small batches in plastic freezer bags and put them in the freezer. And of course, other, less common methods of preservation are appropriate to particular types of herb – in oil, in herb vinegar, sugared and crystallized, and in pickles.

Freshly picked garlic ready for drying off

PESTS AND DISEASES

Herbs are probably no more or less prone to pest and disease problems than any other types of garden plant, although the fact that most are not grown principally for their flowers (which also tend to be small) means that flower problems are perhaps less significant. And although the leaves of many are used in culinary or medicinal applications, it generally matters little if the odd hole happens to be present. Nonetheless, the same overall principles apply to herbs as to any other garden plants: prevention is better than cure but there are limits to how reliable it can be. There are chemical and non-chemical ways of combatting problems, not always of equal effectiveness but the decision on how important a particular problem is and how much damage is tolerable is very much a personal one.

There is, however, an additional factor to bear in mind in relation to control measures. I prefer not to use chemicals at all on edible plants, but since this is not always possible, I have suggested only those products that I think are the safest in respect of the minimum period that must elapse between application and use of the plants. Wherever the option exists, moreover, I have suggested biological control measures, an increasing number of which are being made available to the amateur gardener. So far, those of relevance to the herb garden are a bacterial spray for the control of caterpillars, and two different systems based on beneficial nematodes (eelworms), one of which attacks the larvae of the vine weevil and the other, slugs. The methods of using the nematode techniques, in particular, will be rather different from the procedures you will be used to with chemicals so do read the manufacturers' directions carefully.

In the tables on p.22-4 I have given a simple key to symptoms to enable you to identify easily the most common problems that may be encountered in the herb garden, together with a summary of my recommended control measures and details of the various chemicals available.

Carrot motley dwarf virus on parsley

Alfalfa mosaic virus on coriander

PESTS AND DISEASES

SYMPTOMS ON LEAVES

PROBLEM	DETAIL	PROBABLE CAUSE
Wilting	General	Short of water Root pests or disease Wilt disease
Holed	Generally ragged	Small pests (millepedes, woodlice) Capsid bugs
	Elongate holes; usually with slime present	Slugs or snails
	Fairly large holes over entire leaf or confined to edges	Caterpillars Beetles
Discoloured	Black	Sooty mould
	Predominantly red	Short of water
	More or less bleached	Fertilizer deficiency Short of water Too much water
	Irregular yellowish patterns	Virus
	Irregular tunnels	Leaf miners
	Surface flecking	Leafhoppers
	Brown (scorched) in spring	Frost
Spotted	Brownish, irregular, no mould	Leaf spot
	Small, dusty, brown, black or bright yellow-orange coloured	Rust
Mouldy	Black	Sooty mould
	Grey, fluffy	Grey mould
	White, (or rarely brown), velvety	Mildew
Infested with insects	White, moth-like, tiny	Whiteflies
	Green, grey, black or other colour	Aphids
	Flat, encrusted, like limpets	Scale insects
	Large, six legs, worm-like	Caterpillars
Cobwebs present	Leaves also discoloured	Red spider mites

SYMPTOMS ON FLOWERS

PROBLEM	DETAIL	PROBABLE CAUSE
Drooping	General	Short of water End of flowering period
Tattered	Masses of tiny holes	Caterpillars
	Large pieces torn away	Birds
Removed entirely	Usually discarded nearby	Birds
Discoloured	Powdery white covering	Mildew
Mouldy	Fluffy grey mould	Grey mould

SYMPTOMS ON STEMS OR BRANCHES

PROBLEM	DETAIL	PROBABLE CAUSE
Eaten through	On young plants	Slugs or snails
	On older plants	Mice, voles, rabbits
Infested with insects	Green, grey, black or other colour	Aphids
	Flat, encrusted, like limpets	Scale insects
	Large, six legs, worm-like	Caterpillars
Rotten	At base, young plants	Stem and foot rot
	On shrubby herbs	Decay fungus
Dying back	General	Short of water Coral spot Root pest or disease

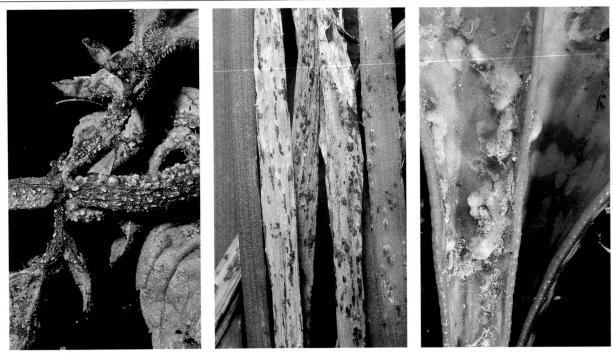

Mint rust   **Rust on chives**   **Mealy bug on aloe**

SOME FUNGICIDES, INSECTICIDES AND PESTICIDAL CHEMICALS USEFUL FOR CONTROLLING PROBLEMS ON HERBS

FUNGICIDES	USES AND COMMENTS
Benomyl Carbendazim Thiophanate-methyl	Systemic[†], for most foliage and stem diseases, including mildew and grey mould
Myclobutanil	Systemic, especially useful for leaf spots and rust
Propiconazole	Systemic, especially useful for leaf spots and rust
Triforine	Systemic, many foliage diseases
Sulphur*	Non-systemic, many foliage diseases

INSECTICIDES	USES AND COMMENTS
Dimethoate	Systemic, most pests
Derris*	Contact, most pests
Natural soaps*	Contact, most pests
Permethrin	Contact, most pests
Pirimicarb	Contact, specific to aphids
Pyrethrum*	Contact, most pests

INSECTICIDES	USES AND COMMENTS
Tar oil	Contact, use in dormant season only on large, deciduous, shrubby herbs to kill overwintering pests on bark

SLUG AND SNAIL KILLERS	USES AND COMMENTS
Methiocarb	As pellets
Metaldehyde	As pellets, mini-pellets or liquid

*Generally acceptable to organic gardeners
[†]Systemic substances are absorbed by the plant and require less frequent and less accurate spraying than contact materials

NB: It should be noted that some of these chemicals are only available in particular formulations or in combination with certain other chemicals. Some may also be marketed for specific pest or disease problems only. In every case, you must read the label directions carefully to be sure that the product is being used for the purpose and in the manner for which it is intended. The names given in this chart are those of the active chemical ingredients. These will not be the same as the product names but will be found printed on the product label. See my comments in the text concerning the use of chemicals on edible plants.

PESTS AND DISEASES

TREATMENTS FOR COMMON PEST AND DISEASE PROBLEMS ON HERBS

PROBLEM	TREATMENT
Aphids	Use a proprietary contact insecticide; pick off affected shoots by hand or wash off insects with hose
Beetles	Normally, treatment is not necessary or justified but in cases of extensive attack use a proprietary contact insecticide
Birds	Erect netting or other protection; in really severe cases, erect bird scarers but remember that all birds enjoy legal protection and may not be harmed
Capsid bugs	The insects are too unpredictable and erratic in occurrence to make any treatment feasible
Caterpillars	Pick off by hand if the caterpillars can be found and are present in small numbers. If masses of insects occur, pick off and destroy entire affected leaves or try biological control (see text)
Coral spot	Cut away and destroy affected branches or twigs, cutting well into the healthy wood
Fertilizer deficiency	Give general balanced liquid fertilizer
Fungal decay	Destroy affected parts or entire plants; no other treatment is feasible
Grey mould	Destroy affected parts; spray with sulphur or systemic fungicide
Leaf hopper	The insects are too erratic and unpredictable to make any treatment practicable
Leaf miner	Remove and destroy affected leaves
Leaf spot	In most instances no treatment is necessary for leaf spot diseases are rarely severe. Where attacks appear to be related to general poor growth however, replace plants
Mice	Set traps or use proprietary poison baits
Mildew	Ensure that plants are not allowed to become too dry and apply systemic fungicide or sulphur
Millepedes	Dust in affected area with derris
Rabbits	The only sure protection is by using a wire netting fence with the lower edge turned outwards at 90° over the soil surface

PROBLEM	TREATMENT
Red spider mites	No treatment is really feasible although keeping plants well watered and mulched will help limit the impact of attacks
Root pests	Normally, no treatment is feasible but with severe and persistent attacks, dust around affected plants with derris. For vine weevil, use biological control (see text)
Root disease	Destroy severely affected plants
Rust	No treatment possible on edible herbs; spray others with propiconazole fungicide
Scale insects	Spray or drench with systemic insecticide
Slugs	Use proprietary slug pellets or liquid controls or homemade remedies such as traps baited with beer. Surround the base of plants with fine powders such as ash or soot or a low barrier of finely spiny twigs such as gorse. Or try biological control (see text)
Snails	If serious, use methods recommended for slugs but generally they are less serious and fewer in number and can be combatted by collecting them by hand and by locating and eradicating them from their hiding places
Sooty mould	Wash off mould with water or destroy badly affected leaves and then identify and treat the insect pest responsible for the honeydew on which the mould grows
Stem and foot rot	Little can be done but as it is often associated with waterlogging, improve drainage of the affected area.
Virus	Effects are usually mild, so no treatment is necessary
Voles	Set mouse traps or use proprietary poison baits
Whiteflies	No treatment is feasible on outdoor plants
Wilt disease	Replace affected plants
Woodlice	Dust plants with derris and locate and eradicate pests from their hiding places

HABITS OF RECOMMENDED HERBS

Achillea millefolium Yarrow **Herbaceous perennial**
Acorus calamus Sweet flag **Herbaceous rhizomatous perennial**
Agastache foeniculum Anise hyssop **Herbaceous perennial**
Agrimonia eupatoria Agrimony **Herbaceous perennial**
Ajuga reptans Bugle **Herbaceous perennial**
Alchemilla vulgaris Lady's mantle **Herbaceous perennial**
Alliaria petiolata Jack-by-the-hedge, Garlic mustard **Biennial**
Aloe vera **Herbaceous perennial**
Aloysia triphylla (syn. *Lippia citriodora*) Lemon verbena **Shrubby perennial**
Allium Herb onions **Bulbous perennials**
Althaea officinalis Marsh mallow **Herbaceous perennial**
Anchusa officinalis Bugloss, Alkanet **Herbaceous perennial**
Anethum graveolens Dill **Biennial**
Angelica archangelica Garden angelica **Biennial/Herbaceous perennial**
Anthriscus cerefolium Chervil **Annual**
Apium graveolens Wild celery, Smallage **Biennial**
Armoracia rusticana Horseradish **Herbaceous perennial**
Arnica montana Arnica **Herbaceous perennial**
Atriplex hortensis Orache **Hardy annual**
Artemisia **Herbaceous perennial**
Bellis perennis Daisy **Herbaceous perennial**
Borago officinalis Borage **Annual**
Brassica species Mustards **Annual**
Calamintha grandiflora Calamint **Herbaceous perennial**
Calendula officinalis Pot marigold **Annual**
Cardamine pratensis Lady's smock, Cuckoo Flower **Herbaceous perennial**
Carthamus tinctorius Safflower, False saffron **Annual**
Carum carvi Caraway **Biennial**
Cedronella canariensis Balm of Gilead **Herbaceous perennial**
Chamaemelum nobile Chamomile **Herbaceous perennial**
Chenopodium bonus-henricus Good King Henry **Herbaceous perennial**
Cichorium intybus Chicory **Herbaceous perennial**
Claytonia perfoliata Winter purslane, Miner's lettuce **Annual**
Coriandrum sativum Coriander **Annual**
Dianthus spp. Pinks **Herbaceous perennial**
Dictamnus albus White dittany, Burning bush **Herbaceous perennial**
Echium vulgare Viper's bugloss **Biennial**
Equisetum arvense Field horsetail **Herbaceous perennial**
Eruca vesicaria Salad rocket, Arugula **Annual**
Eryngium maritimum Sea holly **Herbaceous perennial**
Eupatorium purpureum Trumpet weed **Herbaceous perennial**
Euphrasia officinalis Eyebright **Annual**
Filipendula ulmaria Meadowsweet **Herbaceous perennial**
Foeniculum vulgare Fennel **Herbaceous perennial**
Fragaria vesca Wild strawberry **Herbaceous perennial**
Galega officinalis Goat's rue **Herbaceous perennial**
Galium Woodruff, Bedstraw **Herbaceous perennial**
Genista tinctoria Dyer's greenweed **Shrubby perennial**
Glycyrrhiza glabra Liquorice **Herbaceous perennial**
Helianthus annuus Sunflower **Annual**
Helichrysum italicum (syn. *H. angustifolium*) Curry plant **Shrubby/Herbaceous perennial**
Hesperis matronalis Sweet rocket **Herbaceous perennial/Biennial**
Humulus lupulus Hop **Herbaceous perennial climber**
Hydrastis canadensis Yellow root, Golden seal **Herbaceous perennial**
Hypericum perforatum St John's wort **Shrubby/Herbaceous perennial**
Hyssopus officinalis Hyssop **Shrubby/Herbaceous perennial**
Inula helenium Elecampane **Herbaceous perennial**
Iris florentina Orris root **Herbaceous perennial**
Lamium spp. Dead-nettles **Herbaceous perennial**
Lavandula spp. Lavender **Woody perennial**
Levisticum officinale Lovage **Herbaceous perennial**
Lilium candidum Madonna lily **Bulbous perennial**
Linum usitatissimum Flax **Annual**
Lonicera caprifolium Perfoliate, Honeysuckle **Perennial climber**
Lupinus polyphyllus Lupin **Herbaceous perennial**
Malva moschata Musk mallow **Herbaceous perennial**
Marrubium vulgare Horehound **Herbaceous perennial**
Melilotus officinalis Melilot **Biennial**

Melissa officinalis Lemon balm **Herbaceous perennial**
Monarda didyma Bergamot, Bee balm, Oswego tea **Herbaceous perennial**
Mentha spp. Mint **Herbaceous perennial**
Myosotis spp. Forget-me-not **Annual/Herbaceous perennial**
Myrrhus odorata Sweet cicely **Herbaceous perennial**
Myrtus communis Myrtle **Shrub**
Nepeta cataria Catmint **Herbaceous perennial**
Ocimum basilicum Basil **Annual**
Oenothera biennis Evening primrose **Biennial**
Onobrychis viciifolia Sainfoin **Herbaceous perennial**
Onopordon acanthium Cotton thistle **Biennial**
Origanum spp. Marjoram and Oregano **Herbaceous perennial**
Papaver spp. Poppy **Annual**
Pelargonium spp. Scented pelargonium **Tender perennial**
Petroselinum crispum Parsley **Biennial**
Pimpinella anisum Aniseed **Annual**
Polygonum (syn. *Persicaria*) Bistort, bistorta **Herbaceous perennial**
Portulaca oleracea Summer purslane **Annual**
Primula spp. Primrose, Cowslip **Herbaceous perennial**
Pulmonaria spp. Lungwort **Herbaceous perennial**
Reseda luteola Weld **Biennial**
Rosmarinus officinalis Rosemary **Shrub**
Rubia tinctoria Madder **Herbaceous perennial**
Rumex acetosa Sorrel **Herbaceous perennial**
Ruta graveolens Rue **Shrubby perennial**
Sanguisorba minor Salad burnet **Herbaceous perennial**
Salvia spp. Sage **Shrubby perennial**
Santolina spp. Cotton lavender **Shrubby perennial**
Saponaria officinalis Soapwort **Herbaceous perennial**
Satureja spp. Savory **Shrubby perennial/Annual**
Scutellaria lateriflora Skullcap **Herbaceous perennial**
Sempervivum tectorum Houseleek **Herbaceous perennial**
Sesamum indicum Sesame **Annual**
Sium sisarum Skirret **Herbaceous perennial**
Smyrnium olusatrum Alexanders **Herbaceous perennial**
Stachys officinalis Betony **Herbaceous perennial**
Stellaria media Chickweed **Annual**
Symphytum officinale Comfrey **Herbaceous perennial**
Tagetes patula French marigold **Annual**
Taraxacum officinale Dandelion **Herbaceous perennial**
Tanacetum spp. **Herbaceous perennial**
    Tanacetum balsamita Alecost
    Tanacetum cineariifolium Pyrethrum
    Tanacetum parthenium Feverfew
Thymus spp. Thyme **Shrubby perennial**
Trigonella foenum-graecum Fenugreek **Annual**
Tropaeolum majus Nasturtium **Annual**
Tussilago farfara Coltsfoot **Herbaceous perennial**
Urtica dioica Stinging nettle **Herbaceous perennial**
Valeriana officinalis Valerian **Herbaceous perennial**
Verbascum thapsus Mullein **Biennial**
Verbena officinalis Vervain **Herbaceous perennial**
Vinca major Periwinkle **Herbaceous/Shrubby perennial**
Viola odorata Sweet violet **Herbaceous perennial**
Buxus sempervirens Box **Shrub/Small tree**
Eucalyptus spp. Gum tree **Tree**
Gaultheria procumbens Wintergreen **Shrub**
Ilex aquifolium Holly **Shrub/Tree**
Hamamelis virginiana Witch hazel **Shrub/Small tree**
Laurus nobilis Sweet bay **Shrub/Small tree**
Morus nigra Black mulberry **Tree**
Myrica gale Bog myrtle **Shrub**
Populus balsamifera Balsam poplar **Tree**
Prunus dulcis Almond **Tree**
Quercus spp. Oak **Tree**
Rubus fruticosus Bramble **Shrub**
Rosa spp. Rose **Shrub**
Taxus baccata Yew **Tree**
Vitex agnus-castus Monk's pepper **Tree**

ACHILLEA

Achillea millefolium Yarrow

I have mixed feelings about yarrow, having spent a couple of years eradicating it from my lawn (which I did very successfully with selective weedkiller). There are also cultivated border varieties in colours that I find less than appealing but, nonetheless, if yarrow is grown in its unaltered form in the herb garden, its silver-tinted and very finely divided, almost feathery foliage (hence millefolium – thousand leaves) has its attractions.

HERBAL INTEREST
Culinary Leaves can be used chopped finely as a rather hot, peppery garnish.
Non-culinary Numerous, including cosmetic uses, as a treatment for digestive and other problems and for skin inflammation, although excessive use may render skin sensitive to the sunlight.

CULTIVATION AND CARE
Mulch lightly in autumn and spring, and give a light dressing of a balanced general fertilizer in spring. Cut back dead flower heads or alternatively cut while the plant is in flower and then dry these flower heads for ornamental use. Propagation of the plant is by division in spring or by seed sown in a light, soil-based compost in an unheated propagator in the late spring.
PROBLEMS
None.

ORNAMENTAL APPEAL
Feathery, silvery-grey foliage and a head of small white, daisy-like flowers in summer. Some of the border forms have flower heads of other colours.
SITE AND SOIL Full sun to very light shade, most soils including fairly dry and poor sites but best in good, rich, well drained loams.
HARDINESS Very hardy, tolerating -20°C (-4°F) or below.
SIZE Varies greatly with soil conditions; on a good site, will attain about 75 x 45cm (30 x 18in) after three years.

RECOMMENDED VARIETIES
Normal species only is available.

Achillea millefolium

Acorus calamus Sweet flag

This imposing species is one of the very few common water plants that possess herbal properties and as such is well worth cultivating in larger gardens as a marginal. In common with so many other water-garden species, it is a member of the Arum family, despite the superficial resemblance of its foliage to that of irises. In 'flag' it even shares one of their common names but it is the 'sweet' part of this species' name that earns it an entry here, for the bruised or broken leaves certainly do have a most appealing, sweet and extraordinarily spicy fragrance.

HERBAL INTEREST
Culinary Little in present day cooking but in the past the roots were used to flavour meat.
Non-culinary Dried leaves or rhizome for pot-pourri, the leaves were once used as an aromatic floor covering, and a drug to treat intestinal, kidney and gall-bladder problems (among others) is extracted from the rhizomes.

CULTIVATION AND CARE
Cut down dead foliage and flower stems in autumn or, in cold areas, in the spring. Propagate by division in the spring.
PROBLEMS
None.

AGASTACHE

ORNAMENTAL APPEAL
Iris-like leaves, tiny green-brown flowers in arum-like spikes towards tops of stems in summer.
SITE AND SOIL Full sun or very light shade as water garden marginal in water up to 25cm (10in) deep.
HARDINESS Very hardy, tolerating -20°C (-4°F) or below.
SIZE Will attain about 1.2m x 75cm (4ft x 30in) after four or five years.

RECOMMENDED VARIETIES
The normal species is the usual herb plant although the variety 'Variegatus', with cream and golden leaf stripes is neater and slower growing.

Acorus calamus

Agastache foeniculum Anise hyssop

" *This is one of the lesser known herb in the family Labiatae, possibly because it is North American and possibly because it is less hardy than the more familiar European species. Indeed, unlike its relatives, it is a recent plant in European herb gardens, having been introduced only in the early nineteenth century. It is an attractive, characteristic labiate with a neater clump-forming habit than many, that can easily be grown as a half-hardy perennial in colder areas.* "

HERBAL INTEREST
Culinary Dried leaves can be used as a pleasing aniseed-flavoured infusion.
Non-culinary None.

CULTIVATION AND CARE
In milder areas, mulch lightly in the autumn and spring and give a light dressing of a balanced general fertilizer in spring. Cut back top growth in spring and propagate by division in spring. In cooler areas, take semi-ripe cuttings in summer for overwintering in a cold greenhouse and discard old plants or pot up and keep as stock under cover. The plant tends to be fairly short lived and, even in mild regions, stock should be renewed from cuttings every three years. It can also be raised from seed sown in early summer in an unheated propagator in soil-based compost.

PROBLEMS
Mildew in hot summers.

ORNAMENTAL APPEAL
Typically labiate, nettle-shaped leaves, spikes of small purplish-blue flowers from about mid-summer onwards.
SITE AND SOIL Full sun to very light shade with shelter from cold winds, in light, free-draining but fairly rich soil.
HARDINESS Moderately hardy, tolerating about -10°C (14°F).
SIZE It will grow to attain about 50-75 x 45cm (20-30 x 18in) after three years.

Agastache foeniculum

RECOMMENDED VARIETIES
Normal species is usually available although the rather attractive white-flowered varieties 'Alabaster' and 'Alba' will sometimes be seen. A related, taller but less hardy species, the giant Mexican hyssop, *Agastache mexicana*, is also sometimes offered.

AGRIMONIA

Agrimonia eupatoria Agrimony

❝ *Grown purely as a border ornamental, agrimony is a bit of a disappointment and, in truth, it is rather a feeble-looking thing. It produces very slender spikes of tiny, star-like, yellow flowers during the summer but the drawback is that not only are the stems so slender, but also that rather few of the flowers are ever in bloom at the same time. Nonetheless, having now completed a character assasination, I must add that it is a good plant for attracting bees, it has a sweet perfume (at least, if you can get your nose close enough) and has a long enough history of herbal use to justify its inclusion in a collection. It is, I think, a plant that looks most positively medieval.* ❞

Agrimonia eupatoria

ORNAMENTAL APPEAL
Spikes of small, yellow flowers in summer. Divided leaves, rather reminiscent of meadowsweet, to which it is related.
SITE AND SOIL Full sun, in a wide range of soils provided they are fairly light and well drained.
HARDINESS Very hardy, tolerating -20°C (-4°F) or below.
SIZE Will attain 1-1.2m x 30cm (3-4ft x 12in) after about three or four years.

CULTIVATION AND CARE
Mulch lightly in the autumn and spring and give a light dressing of a balanced general fertilizer in spring. Cut back dead flower heads or alter-

HERBAL INTEREST
Culinary None.
Non-culinary A sweet-scented herbal tea can be made from the leaves and infusions for sore throats, coughs and other complaints. Also yields a yellow dye.

natively cut while in flower and dry to make a honey-scented pot-pourri. Propagate by division in spring or autumn or by seed sown in a light, soil-based compost in an unheated propagator in the spring.

PROBLEMS
None.

RECOMMENDED VARIETIES
Normal species only is available.

Ajuga reptans Bugle

❝ *I like bugle as a striking, ground-cover species for shady places and use it to carpet the area around an old fruit tree in a rather dark part of my own garden. Such a degree of shade tolerance is a considerable virtue in any herb plant, most of which are sun lovers. The deep purple leaves of the best forms contrast superbly with the rich blue flowers in early summer but many people find it too invasive and too mildew prone, and for these reasons it could not really be considered a true gardening classic.* ❞

CULTIVATION AND CARE
Mulch in autumn and spring until well established and give a light dressing of a balanced general fertilizer in spring. Cut back dead flower heads for tidiness and also if mildew sets in. Propagate by division in spring or autumn or by removal of naturally rooted runners.

PROBLEMS
Mildew.

RECOMMENDED VARIETIES
Normal species has green leaves and mid-blue flowers; there are also many varieties but among the more attractive (although no more valuable as herbs) are 'Alba' (white flowers), 'Atropurpurea' (dark purple leaves, dark blue-purple flowers) and 'Burgundy Glow' (leaves slightly variegated, deep red and green).

ALCHEMILLA

Ajuga reptans

HERBAL INTEREST
Culinary None.
Non-culinary Several, including lowering blood pressure, the treatment of bruises and other blood problems.

ORNAMENTAL APPEAL
Short spikes of typically labiate flowers in white, or shades of blue and purple. Variously coloured, more or less oval leaves, ground-covering habit.
SITE AND SOIL Full sun to deep shade but more mildew prone in the sun; in most soils but grows best in fairly rich, organic sites.
HARDINESS Very hardy, tolerating at least -20°C (-4°F) or below.
SIZE Will attain about 15cm x 1m (6in x 3ft) after about four or five years.

Alchemilla vulgaris Lady's mantle

❝ Alchemilla *is high on my list of indispensable garden plants, whether herbal or not. It really is the best and most adaptable herbaceous ground cover but it also has a long and interesting history as a herb. The drops of rain or dew that form, mercury-like, on the foliage were once considered to have magical properties while the 'Lady' of the name is the Virgin Mary, although, coincidentally, many of its medicinal uses were gynaecological. If there is a drawback, it is that it is a bit too successful as ground cover in small gardens although there is a less vigorous and related, alternative species.* ❞

CULTIVATION AND CARE
Cut back dead foliage in late autumn and mulch, then mulch again in early spring and give a balanced general fertilizer. Trim back flower heads as they fade and turn brown. Propagate by division in spring or autumn or by removal of self-sown seedlings.

PROBLEMS
None.

RECOMMENDED VARIETIES
Many plants once called *Alchemilla vulgaris* are now considered to be separate species, but the two forms most generally useful in the herb garden (and sharing herbal properties) are the true
A. vulgaris and the less vigorous, *A. alpina*, which is a good plant for confined space.

HERBAL INTEREST
Culinary Young leaves in small amounts may be added to salads to add a touch of bitterness.
Non-culinary Several medicinal uses for gynaecological disorders, also as a treatment for skin complaints and as a wound healer.

ORNAMENTAL APPEAL
More or less rounded, toothed, light green leaves with feathery heads of yellow-green flowers in early summer. Leaves of A. *alpina* are more strongly divided and finger-like.
SITE AND SOIL Full sun to moderate shade, in most soils but intolerant of very heavy and cold conditions and best on slightly alkaline sites.
HARDINESS Very hardy, tolerating -20°C (-4°F) or below.
SIZE The true A. *mollis* will attain about 50 x 50cm (20 x 20in) after three years; A. *alpina* about half this.

Alchemilla vulgaris

ALLIARIA

Alliaria petiolata Jack-by-the-hedge, Garlic mustard

❝ *I have a very special affection for this plant, although oddly enough, not for its own sake. My liking is really for* Anthocharis cardamines, *the orange-tip butterfly, my favourite native species whose caterpillars have* Alliaria *as their food. Both are among the most welcome sights of early spring although the orange-tip is a member of the same family as the large white, scourge of cabbages; and* Alliaria *is of the same family as the cabbage itself, so the circle is completed. Despite this, Jack-by-the-hedge is a worthy herb plant and is sadly one of the less appreciated of the native culinary species.* ❞

ORNAMENTAL APPEAL
Spikes of rather short-lived white flowers in the early spring, and broad, more or less heart-shaped leaves.
SITE AND SOIL Light to moderate shade, in most soils, tolerant of fairly high moisture.
HARDINESS Very hardy, tolerating -20°C (-4°F) or below.
SIZE Will attain about 75cm-1m x 25cm (30in-3ft x 10in) by its second year.

RECOMMENDED VARIETIES
Normal species only is available.

HERBAL INTEREST
Culinary Chopped leaves make a tangy, slightly onion- or garlic-like addition to salads (the name *Alliaria* is from the same origin as *Allium*), also cooked in various ways, and generally to impart flavour to sauces.
Non-culinary Few medicinal, probably none still used.

CULTIVATION AND CARE
Although it may be a short-lived perennial, it is probably best grown as a biennial; sow the seed initially in pots in spring for planting out in autumn and then allow it to self-seed. Cut down in late summer.
PROBLEMS
None.

Alliaria petiolata

Aloe vera

❝ *I know that you are more likely to think of* Aloe vera *in terms of jars of cream to be found in the bathroom cupboard than of plants to grow in your garden; indeed, I have known more than one person express surprise that the material did actually come from a plant. Yet* Aloe vera *is real enough and one of a huge genus of succulent members of the lily family. Perhaps even more surprising, for a plant that hails from the Mediterranean and similarly warm climates, is that it is a tolerably hardy species although I always think it is best grown in a container that can be moved into some form of shelter if harsh conditions prevail.* ❞

HERBAL INTEREST
Culinary None.
Non-culinary As the basis of skin creams. The sap, when fresh, is applied and used to soothe and heal burned or otherwise damaged skin, but do take heed of the warning under the recommended varieties.

CULTIVATION AND CARE
Best if not mulched as this may give rise to crown-rotting. Water regularly during the summer but allow to dry out between waterings and give liquid fertilizer monthly. In colder areas, move under cover over winter. Propagate by removal of off-sets.
PROBLEMS
Aphids, scale insects, mealybugs.

ALOYSIA

ORNAMENTAL APPEAL
Rosette of tapering, toothed, thick, fleshy, typically succulent, light green leaves, occasionally with a spike of very slender, trumpet-shaped, attractive yellow-orange flowers.

SITE AND SOIL
Full sun, sheltered from cold winds, in free-draining, fertile soil, low in organic matter. In pots, in a good quality soil-based potting compost.

HARDINESS
Fairly to moderately hardy, tolerating about -10°C (14°F).

SIZE
Will attain about 30 x 30cm (12 x 12in) within five years.

RECOMMENDED VARIETIES
Normal species only is available, but be warned that many other *Aloe* species are sold and grown as ornamentals. Some contain astringent sap, very different from that of *A. vera*.

Aloe vera

Aloysia triphylla (syn. *Lippia citriodora*) Lemon verbena

❝ *This isn't the only herb with a strong lemon or citrus scent, but it is probably the one with the strongest. It is native to warm areas of South America but has been grown in Europe for around 200 years as a source of fragrant oil. Although it belongs to the same family as the ornamental verbena of many a summer hanging-basket, it is in a different genus and is certainly a much less ornamental plant.* ❞

Aloysia triphylla

CULTIVATION AND CARE
Mulch in the autumn to protect from winter frost, and then again in spring. Give a balanced general fertilizer in spring and cut out any frost-damaged shoots. May also be fan-trained on a wall in the milder areas when the warmth reflected from the wall brings out the strong perfume. In cooler regions, grow in containers and then move under cover of a cold greenhouse in winter. Propagate by

HERBAL INTEREST
Culinary Leaves may be used for a herbal tea and also chopped to add lemon flavour to desserts and confectionery.
Non-culinary Numerous medical applications, especially in infusions, also as the basis of skin creams and, predictably, in pot-pourri.

ORNAMENTAL APPEAL
Fairly slight, small, pale reddish flowers in loose spikes in late summer, and elongated, dark green leaves.

SITE AND SOIL
Full sun, sheltered from cold winds, in free-draining, fertile soil, preferably slightly alkaline. In pots, in a good quality, soil-based potting compost.

HARDINESS
Fairly to moderately hardy, tolerating about -10°C (14°F).

SIZE
Varies considerably with site; in mild areas, will attain about 3 x 2m (10 x 7ft) within five years; in cooler areas, perhaps one-third of this.

RECOMMENDED VARIETIES
Normal species only is available.

softwood cuttings in early summer in a covered propagator with some slight bottom heat.

PROBLEMS
None.

ALLIUM

Allium Herb onions

❝ A friend who is both a good gardener and cook considers onions the most valuable vegetables in the garden; and I'm not sure that I'd disagree. But this is a herb book and so I shall concentrate here on those members of this large and interesting genus that play a more subsidiary role in the kitchen and/or are interesting plants in their own right.

Some have medicinal value and several are of good ornamental value, too. The genus Allium, of course, is a bulbous one and it is the bulb of the onion itself and some of the other species that is eaten, so the plants are grown as annuals. But for others, it is the foliage and flowers that are used and so these types can be grown as true perennials. ❞

CULTIVATION AND CARE

All of the herb onions are best bought as plants. The old top growth should be cut down to soil level in autumn, the plants mulched lightly then and again in spring when they should also be given a light dressing of some balanced general fertilizer. Propagate by division in spring or autumn or by the removal and planting of the stem bulbils.

PROBLEMS

Rust (especially on chives), mildew, onion flies, white rot.

Allium schoenoprasum

Allium cepa proliferum

ORNAMENTAL APPEAL

Fresh green leaves and stems topped by usually spherical heads of mauve or white flowers. The chive especially is a very attractive plant, while the tree onion has an undeniable appeal in its oddness.

SITE AND SOIL Full sun to very light shade; rich, organic but well drained soil will produce the best plant but most alliums will tolerate poorer soils too, although all resent heavy, waterlogged conditions.

HARDINESS Very hardy, tolerating -20°C (-4°F) or below.

SIZE Varies considerably with species and variety from about 25 x 10cm (10 x 4in) for chives to 1m x 20-30cm (3ft x 8-12in) after two or three years for the tree onions.

HERBAL INTEREST

Culinary Chopped leaves can be used as a more or less strongly flavoured addition (depending on the species) to salads, soups and cooked dishes. Bulbs or bulbils, whole or chopped, cooked or raw, are used in the same manner as onions. Flowers are edible also and have a milder flavour than bulbs or leaves; they make attractive additions to salads and as other garnishes.

Non-culinary Most alliums, particularly garlic, are recognized for their antibiotic properties and many people eat garlic regularly to ward off colds. It is also widely used for its capacity to reduce serum cholesterol levels.

Allium tuberosum

Allium fistulosum

RECOMMENDED VARIETIES

There are a number of closely related *Allium* species, most of which originate from eastern Europe and western Asia although several garden forms are unknown in the wild state. The onion (both bulb and salad or 'spring onion' varieties) and the multi-bulbed shallot are forms of *A. cepa,* but there is an intriguing herb-garden variety of this species called *proliferum*, the tree or Egyptian onion, with large, shallot-sized bulbils produced at the stem tips among the flowers of the inflorescence.

A. sativum is garlic which tends to be grown solely for its clustered bulbs or 'cloves' but which does have perfectly edible foliage too and, in most parts of Britain, may be left to overwinter in the ground as a perennial.

A. scorodoprasum is the giant garlic or rocambole which, although larger than the common garlic, has a milder flavour and produces edible stem tip bulbils.

A. schoenoprasum is the chive, the most familiar and useful herb onion, which produces little if any bulb and is grown solely for its foliage although the flowers are edible too.

A. tuberosum is the Chinese chive, with a tuberous rather than bulbous root, flat, leek-like leaves, white flowers and a mild garlic flavour.

A. fistulosum is the Welsh or bunching onion, and although a vegetable rather than a herb species, it is worth mentioning as it too may be grown as a perennial as it produces a mass of onions at soil level for harvesting throughout the year.

ALTHAEA

Althaea officinalis Marsh mallow

" *I would wager that the first thing that comes to mind for most people when you say the name marshmallow is a sweet, rather sticky confection. Very few would know that it obtained its name and, originally, its stickiness and sweetness from a species of the mallow that happens to grow in marshes. Today, marshmallows, the confection, are made from other ingredients but the plant remains an interesting addition to a herb garden collection. In reality, salt marshes are its natural home but it is an adaptable plant and will grow in a wide range of soil types.* "

Althaea officinalis

RECOMMENDED VARIETIES
Normal species only is available.

HERBAL INTEREST
Culinary Chopped leaves and flowers can be used as a rather sweet addition to salads. Leaves may also be lightly boiled or steamed as a vegetable and roots par-boiled, then chopped and fried.
Non-culinary Numerous uses, including infusions for coughs and sore throats and also to reduce external inflammation.

ORNAMENTAL APPEAL
Moderate interest only: spikes of rather dull, velvety leaves with pale pink, typical mallow flowers borne in the axils.
SITE AND SOIL
Full sun, in most soils provided they are fairly moist.
HARDINESS
Very hardy, tolerating -20°C (-4°F) or below.
SIZE
Will attain about 2m x 50cm (7ft x 20in) within three years.

CULTIVATION AND CARE
Mulch in autumn and spring and give a light dressing of balanced general fertilizer in the spring. Cut down in autumn. Propagate by division in autumn or spring or by seed, sown in spring in a soil-based compost.
PROBLEMS
I would have expected the devastating disease hollyhock rust to attack marsh mallows but I have never actually seen it do so.

Anchusa officinalis Bugloss, Alkanet

" *Not to be confused with Viper's bugloss (p.52), nor with bugle (p.28), this is a native British plant with an old use revealed by its alternative name of alkanet, derived from an ancient Arabic word for henna. It was commonly grown as a source of the red henna dye, although, to confuse matters, henna was also obtained from other boraginaceous plants, also known as alkanets. Its appearance is rather typical of many of its family in that it is a very predictable, uninspiring and rather unexciting plant.* "

HERBAL INTEREST
Culinary Chopped leaves and flowers can be used as an addition to salads.
Non-culinary Apart from a source of dye, extracts of the roots have been put to various medicinal uses.

CULTIVATION AND CARE
Mulch in autumn and spring and give a light dressing of balanced general fertilizer in the spring. Cut down in autumn. Propagate by division in autumn or spring or by seed, sown in spring in a soil-based compost. May also be grown quite succesfully as a biennial.
PROBLEMS
None.

ANETHUM

ORNAMENTAL APPEAL

Small purplish-blue flowers in characteristic, curling spikes, leaves narrowly elongated and, unlike many bristly members of the family, these are rather softly hairy.

SITE AND SOIL
Best in full sun and on rather light, free-draining soils; unlikely to succeed on very wet or cold sites.

HARDINESS
Very hardy, tolerating -20°C (-4°F) or below.

SIZE
Will attain about 1m x 50cm (3ft x 20in) within about two years.

RECOMMENDED VARIETIES
Normal species only is available.

Anchusa officinalis

Anethum graveolens Dill

❝ *Dill is one of the trickiest and most frustrating of the common umbelliferous herbs. It has become better known recently because of the popularity of the jars of pickled cucumbers to which dill is added as a flavouring. These are generally imported from rather warm parts of Eastern Europe and other areas, and this is the clue to the problem. It isn't a British native and thrives best in conditions that we find hard to provide. If all else fails, then fennel (p.57) is a stronger-flavoured but definitely much easier substitute.* ❞

Anethum graveolens

CULTIVATION AND CARE
Grow as a half-hardy annual, sowing seed in growing positions in spring and thinning to 30cm (12in) between plants. If more than one row is needed, space rows 60cm (24in) apart. The best plan is to sow a few seeds in mid-spring under cloches to provide plants for seeding in late summer. Then sow a few more successionally into summer to give a regular supply of fresh young foliage. Pick leaves and flower heads fresh, and seedheads before seeds fully ripen, and then allow them to dry naturally. Take care not to allow the plants to become very dry between waterings or to suffer any other checks to growth.

PROBLEMS
None.

RECOMMENDED VARIETIES
Normal species only is available.

HERBAL INTEREST

Culinary Chopped leaves can be used to flavour cooked fish, cream cheese, soups and other dishes. Seed is used with fish, soups and some confections. Flower heads are added to pickled cucumbers and other pickled vegetables. Seeds and flower heads used to make dill vinegar.
Non-culinary Various, principally dill water for digestion.

ORNAMENTAL APPEAL
Delicate, feathery, green foliage, umbels of small yellow flowers.

SITE AND SOIL
Full sun, in light, free-draining but fertile soil. Will never succeed in cold or wet situations.

HARDINESS
Fairly hardy, tolerating about 0-10°C (14°F) but almost invariably grown as an annual.

SIZE
Will attain about 60cm-1m x 50cm (24in-3ft x 20in) in British summer conditions.

ANGELICA

Angelica archangelica Garden angelica

❝ The range of flavours offered by the family Umbelliferae never ceases to amaze me. What greater contrast could there be, for instance, between the assertive aniseed of fennel and the gentle sweetness of angelica? Although there are British species of Angelica, the best and most widely grown herb plant is a European, found wild here only where it has escaped from its centuries-old cultivation. Like many another umbellifer, it is a white-flowered plant of damp places but it falls into the more robust group with less finely divided leaves and with stout stems. ❞

Angelica archangelica

RECOMMENDED VARIETIES
Normal species only is available.

HERBAL INTEREST
Culinary Stems are crystallized for decorating confectionery, leaves are used in compotes of rhubarb and other fruits to reduce tartness, seeds to flavour gin and other drinks.

Non-culinary Several minor medicinal uses, including an infusion as a treatment for flatulence; also roots and other parts are used as a source of pleasant, sweet aromas (the development of these two uses is to be considered purely coincidental).

ORNAMENTAL APPEAL
No special distinction to separate it from other umbellifers; umbels of small, greenish-white flowers held above its large, light green leaves.

SITE AND SOIL Partial shade, in moist, preferably organic soils.

HARDINESS Very hardy, tolerating -20°C (-4°F) or below.

SIZE Will attain about 2m x 75cm (7ft x 30in) by second year.

CULTIVATION AND CARE
Best grown as a biennial, sowing seed in growing positions in spring. Cut down to soil level in autumn then mulch. Mulch again in spring and give a light dressing of balanced general fertilizer. Harvest leaves in early summer, then stems for crystallizing and, finally, seedheads in late summer.

PROBLEMS
None.

Anthriscus cerefolium Chervil

❝ Chervil is an annual, domestic relative of that most common of wild umbellifers throughout much of the British Isles, the white-flowered cow parsley, Anthriscus sylvestris. The foliage is very similar, although chervil is a much shorter-growing plant, and while cow parsley has no garden virtues, chervil is a valuable species with one of the more elusive herbal flavours. I have heard it variously described as aniseed, myrrh and parsley, but personally find it like none of these and curiously unique. It has long been appreciated by French chefs and reference to cerfeuil will often be found on French menus. ❞

HERBAL INTEREST
Culinary Chopped leaves are used in salads and with a wide range of cooked dishes such as chicken and many fish that do not themselves have strong flavours.

Non-culinary Several minor medicinal uses, usually raw leaves for digestive well-being.

CULTIVATION AND CARE
Grow as hardy annual, sowing in growing positions under cloches in mid-spring, thinning plants to about 20cm (8in) spacing. May be allowed to self-seed if space allows.

PROBLEMS
None.

APIUM

ORNAMENTAL APPEAL
Pretty, very finely divided leaves and white flower heads with a rather neat overall habit.
SITE AND SOIL Light shade, in light, moist, but definitely free-draining soils.
HARDINESS Moderately hardy, tolerating about -10°C (14°F).
SIZE Attains 30-45 x 30cm (12-18 x 12in) within a year.

RECOMMENDED VARIETIES
Normal species only is available.

Anthriscus cerefolium

Apium graveolens Wild celery, Smallage

❝ *The cultivated varieties of celery are now among the less commonly grown kitchen garden vegetables, largely because the trenched types require rich organic soil and considerable care and attention, while the self-blanching types have little to commend them. But in a large herb garden, space should be found for the wild plant which has a long and interesting history stretching back to classical times when it was used, along with olives, parsley and other plants, to make wreathes for the victors in the ancient Greek games.* ❞

HERBAL INTEREST
Culinary Seed is used to make celery salt; chopped leaves in salads and with a number of cooked dishes, especially fish.
Non-culinary Used historically for medicinal purposes, and now known to have a very high vitamin content.

CULTIVATION AND CARE
Grow as a hardy annual or a biennial, sowing in growing positions in mid-spring and then thinning plants to about 35-45cm (14-18in) spacing. May flower and seed in the first year but if not, mulch in the autumn, give a little balanced fertilizer in spring and wait until the second summer to harvest the seeds.

PROBLEMS
Fungal leaf spot.

Apium graveolens

ORNAMENTAL APPEAL
Rather pretty, small, slightly divided leaves and umbels of greenish-white flowers.
SITE AND SOIL Light shade, in rich, moist, but definitely free-draining soils.
HARDINESS Very hardy, tolerating -20°C (-4°F).
SIZE Attains 80cm-1m x 30cm (32in-3ft x 12in) usually by the second year.

RECOMMENDED VARIETIES
Normal species only for herbal interest; cultivated variants if you wish to grow them as vegetables.

ARMORACIA

Armoracia rusticana Horseradish

" There aren't many herbs that can turn on their owners in quite the way that horseradish can. It will even surpass mint in its invasiveness and ineradicability, and really must be kept well confined from the outset. It should, ideally, be planted in a pit lined with bricks or stone slabs, but even these should be mortared together or it will force its way through the joints. Despite my apparent endeavours, however, I do hope that nothing will put you off growing this most valuable culinary plant. If there is no comparison worth making between fresh and dried leaf herbs, then there is certainly none between freshly prepared horseradish sauce and the bland, shop-bought mixture so often used. "

HERBAL INTEREST
Culinary Roots, grated or, even better, minced to make sauce for use with meat and smoked or oily fish. An excellent variant is made by mixing in chopped, cooked beetroot.
Non-culinary Several minor medicinal uses, including a treatment for coughs and other throat complaints.

CULTIVATION AND CARE
The best way to grow horseradish for root production and to keep its vigour within bounds is as an annual. Set aside an area of soil about 75cm x 75cm (30 x 30in), ideally confined

RECOMMENDED VARIETIES
Normal species is widely available but a prettier variant, 'Variegata', with white leaf blotches is sometimes seen and seems to be no different in its culinary value.

ORNAMENTAL APPEAL
Almost none, apart from the variegated form. Large, strap-like, fresh green leaves, small white flowers are produced unpredictably in the late summer on a tall spike.
SITE AND SOIL Almost any; although horseradish grows best in full sun and good soil, any experienced gardener will know that it is perfectly capable of growing anywhere.
HARDINESS Very hardy, tolerating -20°C (-4°F) or below.
SIZE Will attain about 75cm-1m x 30cm (30in-3ft x 12in) within a year if grown, as suggested, as an annual plant.

by stone slabs sunk vertically, and plant two or three plants in spring. Dig up in autumn and either use the roots immediately to make sauce or store them frozen until required. Inevitably, pieces of root will be left in the ground to renew growth in the following year. Give a top-dressing of compost mulch and also balanced general fertilizer in early spring.
PROBLEMS
Leaf-attacking insects although none are that serious, also mildew, club-root (although this is uncommon).

Armoracia rusticana

Arnica montana Arnica

" Arnica is one of those native plants that few people ever see, as it has become something of a rarity, and even fewer can name it; it tends to be dismissed as 'another' yellow-flowered daisy. Yet it is pretty enough in its natural habitat of dry montane grasslands and is pretty, too, in the herb garden where it has been grown for many centuries for various medicinal uses. "

HERBAL INTEREST
Culinary None; it should not be taken internally.
Non-culinary Several minor medicinal uses, especially to produce an external treatment for sprain and strain relief; also for a herbal tobacco produced from the dried roots and foliage.

ATRIPLEX

ORNAMENTAL APPEAL
Downy, hairy leaves in an attractive rosette from which the single, rather lax, yellow daisy flowers arise in summer.
SITE AND SOIL Full sun, in acidic, free-draining but a fairly rich soil.
HARDINESS Very hardy, tolerating -20°C (-4°F) or below.
SIZE Will attain about 50-75 x 30cm (20-30 x 12in) after about four years.

Arnica montana

CULTIVATION AND CARE
Mulch lightly in the spring and autumn and give a light dressing of balanced general fertilizer in spring. Cut down top growth in autumn. Propagate by division in autumn or spring; also by seed sown in spring in a humus-enriched, soil-based compost in a cold-frame.

PROBLEMS
Mildew, but generally after flowering.

RECOMMENDED VARIETIES
Normal species only is available.

Atriplex hortensis Orache

❝ *The large extent of the spinach family, Chenopodiaceae, isn't appreciated by most people nearly as much as that of the cabbage family, Cruciferae, and orache is one of its least familiar members although it has been cultivated in herb gardens for centuries and was once a very important medicinal plant. Like a number of other plants that have passed from favour in Britain, it is still popular in France where it is used as a salad vegetable and basis for soups. There are native species of orache, all more or less acceptable as substitutes for spinach but this, the herbal form, was originally an Asian plant.* ❞

ORNAMENTAL APPEAL
Large, more or less triangular leaves, unspectacular in the plain green-leaved form but striking in the coloured variants. Orache is a large plant, however, and its much-branched habit means that it should be planted with due consideration for its impact. Flowers are tiny and carried in boring, dock-like heads.
SITE AND SOIL Full sun, in free-draining but fairly rich soil.
HARDINESS Very hardy, tolerating -20°C (-4°F) or below.
SIZE Will attain up to 2m x 75cm (7ft x 30in) within a year.

CULTIVATION AND CARE
Sow seed in pots and then transplant at spacings of 60 x 60cm (24 x 24in),

Atriplex hortensis

HERBAL INTEREST
Culinary Strictly speaking, none as a herb although the coloured forms make a very pretty addition to salads.
Non-culinary Once important medicinally for its general healing properties and very widely used as the basis of a treatment for sore throats.

RECOMMENDED VARIETIES
A golden-leaved form and a reddish-purple-leaved variant called *rubra* are sometimes available and look most attractive interplanted alongside the normal green-leaved plant.

alternating coloured-leaf forms if they are available.

PROBLEMS
Mildew, leaf-attacking insects.

ARTEMISIA

Artemisia

66 *Artemisias are among the unsung heroes of the herb garden. They are never really spectacular and, with the best will in the world, most can't truly be described as attractive although there are some striking forms with silver leaves. Yet among them are some of the oldest and most traditional of medicinal herbs as well as, in tarragon, one of the most individual and valuable of culinary plants. The Greeks knew the value of artemisias and the genus is named after no less a personage than the sister of the classical King Mausolus, whom she buried in a magnificent tomb (hence, mausoleum). But despite her no doubt very busy life, Artemisia still found time to grow and study herbs; a lesson for us all.* 99

Artemisia arborescens

Artemisia lactiflora 'Guizhou'

HERBAL INTEREST

Culinary Leaves of tarragon have numerous uses, especially when combined with chicken but also to make tarragon vinegar and herb butter, tartar sauce, hollandaise sauce and other purposes. Other *Artemisia* species are of little culinary value although some have been used to flavour alcoholic drinks, most notably absinthe.

Non-culinary Tarragon has several minor medicinal uses and was once employed as a treatment against scurvy (the plant is now known to be rich in vitamin C). The leaves of other *Artemisia* species are used as a source of insect repellents in homes and gardens; formerly used as a treatment for internal human parasites they also had various minor medicinal uses as general antiseptics.

CULTIVATION AND CARE

Mulch lightly in spring and autumn and give a balanced general fertilizer

ORNAMENTAL APPEAL

Finely divided and aromatic foliage, very silvery in the best selected forms.

SITE AND SOIL Full sun, in light, free-draining, preferably slightly alkaline soil.

HARDINESS Most are more or less hardy, tolerating -15°C (5°F) or below, provided mulch protection is given to the crowns in winter.

SIZE Varies with species; most will attain 90cm-1m x 30-45cm (34in-3ft x 12-18in) within three years; but *A. caucasica* is a low-growing, ground-cover species while *A. lactiflora* tends to be taller than most and can reach 2m (7ft).

in spring. Cut back to a few centimetres above the crown in autumn. Propagate by semi-ripe cuttings in summer, rooted in a soil-based compost in a cold-frame.

PROBLEMS

None.

RECOMMENDED VARIETIES

The best variety, the authentic tarragon, is *Artemisia dracunculus* with narrowly elongated, glossy leaves and a subtle, slightly aniseed-like flavour. The more narrowly leaved, so-called Russian tarragon *A. dracunculoides* is a most inferior plant and no substitute for the former.

A. arborescens is more shrubby than most species with tufted, silvery and soft foliage. *A. abrotanum*, (southernwood, old man or lad's love) has finely divided leaves with a scent of lemon. *A. absinthium*, (wormwood) is an extremely bitter-tasting plant with finely divided leaves; much the most attractive form is the very silvery 'Lambrook Silver' widely grown as an ornamental. *A. caucasica* (also called *A. pedemontana* or *A. lantata*) has very soft, silky and fairly finely divided leaves. *A. lactiflora* (white mugwort) has much less finely divided, toothed, light green leaves. *A. ludoviciana* var. *latiloba*, (western mugwort, white sage) has very willow-like leaves with a silvery sheen, most marked in the ornamental varieties 'Silver Queen' and 'Valerie Finnis'. *A. pontica* (Roman wormwood) has pretty, very feathery foliage and a strong, rather spicy smell.

A. ludoviciana **'Valerie Finnis'**

Artemisia dracunculus

Artemisia abrotanum

BELLIS

Bellis perennis Daisy

" Queries on how to control lawn weeds reach me in predictable numbers every year. Dandelions, clover, speedwell – someone needs an answer to them all; yet very rare is the person who wants his or her lawn freed from Bellis perennis, the little white and golden lawn daisy. Perhaps it is because it's pretty, perhaps because it doesn't spread with quite the aggressiveness of most weeds, or perhaps it's simply that we all have memories of childhood games. None of this explains its presence in a herb garden, however, and yet it really is worth growing for its charming flowers alone which look wonderful in salads. "

RECOMMENDED VARIETIES
The normal species is the one for herb garden use; the selected colour forms and doubles just don't have the same appeal.

ORNAMENTAL APPEAL
Familiar single daisy flowers with white, pink-tipped rays and golden discs; a very neat, rosette habit.
SITE AND SOIL Almost any but best in full sun or very light shade, and least successful on very light, free-draining soils.
HARDINESS Very hardy, tolerating -20°C (-4°F) or below.
SIZE Will attain about 15 x 15cm (6 x 6in) after about two or three years.

HERBAL INTEREST
Culinary Flowers and leaves can be used in salads (but do be sure not to pick them from a lawn that has been treated with weedkiller at any time).
Non-culinary Several minor medicinal uses, the leaves in particular are used to make an external treatment for bruises.

CULTIVATION AND CARE
Very little needed. May be grown as an annual but best as a small perennial group, given a little balanced fertilizer in spring and divided every few years. When it's grown in this manner, you will be surprised how many gardeners fail to recognize it as the same plant that grows on their lawns.

Bellis perennis

PROBLEMS
None.

Borago officinalis Borage

" Borage has given me and my visitors some of our most pleasant herbal experiences, either when we have seen it growing in the garden or when it has been used as a garnish in our cold drinks (see next column). It's also given me the odd frustration, however, for it does self-seed with abandon and seedlings must be pulled out ruthlessly. To my mind, it has much the most attractive flowers in the entire family Boraginaceae and the closer you examine them, the lovelier they are. It is one of the essentials of any herb garden and, understandably, has been admired for centuries and has a considerable associated folklore. "

ORNAMENTAL APPEAL
Beautiful, small, single, pointed flowers of electric-blue.
SITE AND SOIL Prefers either full sun or very light shade and light, free-draining but not at all impoverished soil.
HARDINESS Very hardy, tolerating -20°C (-4°F) or below.
SIZE Will attain about 60-75 x 30cm (24-30 x 12in) within a year or so.

CULTIVATION AND CARE
Sow, in the first instance, in growing positions and then allow to self-sow each year and remove any unwanted seedlings.

PROBLEMS
None.

BRASSICA

Brassica spp. Mustards

❝ For most gardeners, brassicas are vegetables, and, certainly, the genus Brassica *embraces some of the most important crops in the kitchen garden: cabbage, cauliflower, Brussels sprout, kale, to name a few. But there are also the brassicas for which the seeds,* rather than the leaves or flowers, are more important and these, the mustards, should find a place in the herb garden if you have room for them; they are, however, large plants. But try home grown mustard and you will be loathe to buy anything in a bottle again. ❞

HERBAL INTEREST
Culinary Seeds are used to make mustard sauce; use black or brown seeds and grind them into a little cold water. Use white seeds as a preservative in pickles. Young leaves and flowers can also be used to add spiciness to salads, sandwiches and many other savoury dishes.
Non-culinary Various medicinal uses, most notably to produce a healing warm bath for the feet and also used as an emetic to induce vomiting.

ORNAMENTAL APPEAL
Bright yellow, typical *Brassica* flowers in summer.
SITE AND SOIL
Full sun or very light shade and light, free-draining but fertile soil.
HARDINESS
Very hardy, tolerating -20°C (-4°F) or below.
SIZE
Varies considerably with species: white mustard will attain 45-75 x 25cm (18-30 x 10in); black mustard and brown mustard from 1-2m x 75cm (3-7ft x 30in).

CULTIVATION AND CARE
Grow as a hardy annual, sowing seed into growing positions and thin to about 15cm (6in). May self-seed but as they will hybridize freely, it is best to sow fresh using bought or specially saved seed each spring.
PROBLEMS
Leaf-attacking insects, mildew and clubroot.

RECOMMENDED VARIETIES
The naming of many cultivated brassicas is both contentious and very confusing, all the more so since the plants hybridize very readily and because, especially with the vegetable species, the cultivated forms bear little resemblance to any wild plants. There are, however, three important mustard species named, after their seed colours, as white, black and brown and these are generally called *B. hirta*, *B. nigra* and *B. juncea*. *B. nigra* is the true 'mustard and cress' mustard that imparts the tangy flavour.

HERBAL INTEREST
Culinary
Flowers can be used for decoration in salads and, most appealingly, in cold drinks. Add single flowers to the compartments of ice cube trays; when the ice subsequently melts in the glass, the flowers will float out. The young leaves may also be used in salads and, I am told, cooked like spinach but that can apply to many things and it doesn't mean that they will have any taste.
Non-culinary
Several minor medicinal uses, including, again like many other things, a treatment for any external inflammation.

Borago officinalis

RECOMMENDED VARIETIES
The normal species is the one to grow although there is a white form, 'Alba', which seems a rather pointless variant, and also a rather uncommon form with variegated foliage.

CALAMINTHA

Calamintha grandiflora Calamint

" *Labiates and Umbellifers undoubtedly vie for the most important role in the herb garden. This plant is a rather typical labiate in its upright, angled stem, its opposite pairs of leaves and its lipped flowers, but it is very commonly seen as a component of a herbaceous border. There is no apparent reason for this, apart from the fact that the flowers are appealingly bluish instead of the usual labiate insipid mauve. This calamint is from southern Europe and Asia and does have the merit of a pleasing mint-like perfume. For years it has been put to various medicinal uses.* "

HERBAL INTEREST
Culinary None.
Non-culinary The dried leaves are used to make a somewhat peppermint-flavoured tea, said to be good, like so many other things, for the digestion.

ORNAMENTAL APPEAL
Rather little; erect spikes of typically labiate form with bluish flowers in summer.
SITE AND SOIL Light to moderate shade as it is naturally a woodland plant, in free-draining, moderately rich, preferably alkaline soil.
HARDINESS Very hardy, tolerating -20°C (-4°F) or below.
SIZE Will attain about 45 x 30cm (18 x 12in) after two or three years.

CULTIVATION AND CARE
Mulch in spring and autumn and give some balanced general fertilizer in autumn. Cut down all above-ground growth in autumn.
PROBLEMS
None.

RECOMMENDED VARIETIES
The normal species is most usually seen but there is a variegated-leaved form, 'Variegata'.

Calendula officinalis Pot marigold

" *Perhaps my favourite annual herb, this is the traditional marigold as far as I am concerned – the vulgar-flowered African and French newcomers just don't hold a candle to it. It has a simplicity and honesty that allows it to flaunt the most gaudy of orange shades and yet not seem crude. It has been a garden plant for so long that its origins are lost in time but I do believe that nothing else contrasts so happily with the fresh greens of summer salads as these hot, vibrant and flame and amber tones, be they in the garden or in the salad bowl.* "

CULTIVATION AND CARE
Sow seed in growing positions in mid-spring and thin plants to a spacing of about 12cm (5in). Dead head regularly. It's best when it can be allowed to self-seed but this is not successful on all sites and re-sowing each year may be necessary.
PROBLEMS
Mildew, but generally only after flowering is over.

RECOMMENDED VARIETIES
There are many selected forms and mixtures, the modern types including reds and yellows as well as the more familiar clear orange. But for me, nothing beats the taller, pure orange forms like 'Orange King'.

Calamintha grandiflora

CARDAMINE

Calendula officinalis

Cardamine pratensis Lady's smock, Cuckoo flower

❝ There's a small clump of a pretty, little, double pink-flowered plants pressed right into a corner of one of my borders that, I can virtually guarantee, will attract a considerable amount of interest when I have people strolling about my garden. Surprise is the invariable reaction when I announce to them that it is merely the double-flowered form of a common wild plant. There is more surprise when folk see that the single-flowered species is one of the more unexpected inhabitants of my herb garden where it is one of the daintiest of the plants that I grow. ❞

ORNAMENTAL APPEAL
Striking double or semi-double, bright orange flowers on stiff stems with fresh green leaves.
SITE AND SOIL Full sun or very light shade, tolerates most soils but best in none-too-rich, free-draining sites.
HARDINESS Very hardy, tolerating -20°C (-4°F) or below.
SIZE Varies with variety but the better, older forms will attain about 45 x 30cm (18 x 12in) within the year.

HERBAL INTEREST
Culinary Flowers, either whole or as individual florets, are used in salads and also cooked dishes including cheese recipes, soups and omelettes. Leaves are also used in salads.
Non-culinary Various extracts, as well as the raw leaves, have been used to make healing preparations for skin bruises and wounds.

HERBAL INTEREST
Culinary Rather tangy leaves can be added to salads, or are good to nibble, as I do, in the garden.
Non-culinary Various minor medicinal uses, particularly as the basis of a cough remedy and as a source of vitamin C.

CULTIVATION AND CARE
Little needed once the plant is established but it will benefit from a light dressing of any balanced general fertilizer in the spring.

PROBLEMS
Mildew, occasionally clubroot.

RECOMMENDED VARIETIES
The normal, wild species and the double 'Flore Pleno' are equally commonly seen in nurseries and are equally valuable as herbs.

ORNAMENTAL APPEAL
Small, very pale pink flowers and divided leaves in a basal rosette.
SITE AND SOIL Light to moderate shade, in damp, fairly nutrient-rich soil.
HARDINESS Very hardy, tolerating -20°C (-4°F) or below.
SIZE In good growing conditions, it will attain 45-60 x 15cm (18-24 x 6in) after two years.

Cardamine pratensis

CARTHAMUS

Carthamus tinctorius
Safflower, False saffron

66 *Plants prefixed with the name 'false' are either closely related to the real thing or are put to similar uses. In this case it is the latter, for while 'genuine' saffron is produced from a species of* Crocus, *it is very costly and this Asian annual daisy yields a useful substitute. It is naturalized in parts of Britain but both in the wild or in the herb garden, it is a striking ornamental and worth having, even if you don't want home-grown pretend saffron.* 99

RECOMMENDED VARIETIES
Various colour selections are sometimes available but the normal species is the one to choose for herbal use; and it is more attractive too.

CULTIVATION AND CARE
Grow as a more or less hardy annual, raising seedlings under glass in spring, and plant out when they are large enough to handle.

HERBAL INTEREST
Culinary Florets can be used as a substitute for saffron as a food colouring agent; cooking oil is extracted commercially from the seeds of this plant.
Non-culinary Several medicinal uses including seed extracts which have been used to lower blood pressure and flowers are used as the basis of laxatives.

ORNAMENTAL APPEAL
Robust, thistle-like flowers with reddish-orange florets on stems with quite large, bristly leaves.
SITE AND SOIL Full sun, in light, fairly rich but definitely free-draining soil.
HARDINESS Hardy, tolerating about -15°C (-5°F) but immaterial as grown as an annual.
SIZE Will attain about 1m x 30cm (3ft x 12in) within a year.

PROBLEMS
Mildew.

Carthamus tinctorius

Carum carvi
Caraway

66 *I doubt if caraway has ever been more popular in Britain than it is today, for its seeds are recommended in a great many recipes and are readily available at food stores. It is, however, an ancient herb plant and although not a native, has long been naturalized in this country. It is among those plants that always remind you that their natural home is somewhere a little warmer and I find it one of the trickier umbellifers to grow well. In appearance, it is very much like any other, relatively low-growing, white-flowered member of its family, and it is rather closely related to parsley.* 99

HERBAL INTEREST
Culinary Numerous uses for the seeds: as a flavouring in bread and confectionery, in soups and particularly important in Indian and other Asian cookery; also scattered over fattier types of meat and poultry. Roots may be boiled as a vegetable but I find them a bit wiry and uninteresting, and leaves may be used in salads.
Non-culinary Minor medicinal uses, principally to aid digestion but also, just as with parsley, chewing caraway seeds or leaves is pretty effective at killing the smell of garlic on the breath provided it is done fairly promptly after the garlic has been eaten.

CEDRONELLA

Carum carvi

ORNAMENTAL APPEAL
Rather minimal, with feathery foliage and some small white flowers in umbels.
SITE AND SOIL Full sun, in light, fairly rich but free-draining soil.
HARDINESS Hardy, tolerating about -15°C (5°F).
SIZE Will attain about 60 x 20cm (24 x 8in) within two years.

CULTIVATION AND CARE
Grow as a more or less hardy annual but sow seeds in growing positions in spring in rows 15-20cm (6-8in) apart and thin plants to 15cm (6in) spacing. Like most umbellifers, the tap root is easily damaged if transplanted. Do not cut down after first year but harvest the seeds when they are ripe at the end of the second summer.

PROBLEMS
None.

RECOMMENDED VARIETIES
Normal species only is available.

Cedronella canariensis Balm of Gilead

" *Balm of Gilead is one of those names that you imagine only occur within the pages of the Bible and, just as with myrrh and frankincense, it comes as something of a surprise to discover that such things really exist. The true, biblical balm of Gilead is a species of aromatic shrub and this labiate is one of a handful of other species that have acquired the name through having a somewhat similar fragrance. Its romantic name and associations might lead you to expect something rather special but it is a bit of a let-down, being yet another of those rather anonymous labiates, worthy of inclusion in a collection for its perfume, but best planted out of sight.* "

ORNAMENTAL APPEAL
Very slight, with small pinkish flowers in terminal heads, and elongated, dull green leaves. I have seen this plant recommended as a conservatory subject but can't imagine why, apart from the perfume.
SITE AND SOIL Full sun, in light, fairly rich but free-draining soil; or in a good soil-based potting compost in a container.
HARDINESS Barely to fairly hardy, tolerating about -5°C (23°F).
SIZE Will attain about 1m x 30cm (3ft x 12in) within a season, if raised initially in warmth.

HERBAL INTEREST
Culinary None.
Non-culinary Leaves are a source of heavy, sweet perfume.

Cedronella canariensis

CULTIVATION AND CARE
Best grown as a half-hardy annual, sowing seed in warmth in early spring and then growing the plant in a container which can be stood outside once the danger of frost has passed. It should then be discarded because, even as a perennial, it is short-lived.

PROBLEMS
None.

RECOMMENDED VARIETIES
Normal species only is available.

CHAMAEMELUM

Chamaemelum nobile Chamomile

"I'm quite sure that chamomile wouldn't be as popular today if word hadn't passed around that the Queen has a chamomile lawn at Buckingham Palace, even though these 'lawns' have been grown for centuries. But whether or not you aspire to such sophisticated gardening, there's no denying that one of the flowering chamomiles should be in every herb collection. They look good, they smell good and, if all herbalists are to be believed, they do you good, too. "

HERBAL INTEREST
Culinary None.
Non-culinary Flowers are used to produce chamomile tea, said to have all manner of beneficial properties including the prevention of bad dreams. An extract from the flowers is used for conditioning the hair.

ORNAMENTAL APPEAL
Very soft, feathery foliage and low-growing habit above which the small, individual daisy flowers are borne.
SITE AND SOIL Full sun, in quite light, fairly rich but free-draining soil.
HARDINESS Very hardy, tolerating about -20°C (-4°F) but browned in cold winters.
SIZE Will attain about 25 x 30cm (10 x 12in) in three years.

Chamaemelum nobile

CULTIVATION AND CARE
Little needed once plants are established but best divided every three or four years as it tends to turn brown in the centre and die back. Trim off flower heads when fresh if required for pot-pourri or as they fade if not. Give a light dressing of any balanced general fertilizer in spring.

PROBLEMS
None.

RECOMMENDED VARIETIES
The lawn chamomile is 'Treneague', a non-flowering variant of the herb garden species, although the double-flowered form 'Flore Pleno' is lovely and could be chosen for herbal use instead. The rather similar-looking German chamomile, *Matricaria recutita*, with similar uses, is an annual easily raised from seed. There is another daisy, the pretty golden-flowered *Anthemis tinctoria*, known as dyer's chamomile.

Chenopodium bonus-henricus Good King Henry

"I once asked listeners to a radio programme to write and tell me how this plant obtained its name and which King Henry was being honoured. The suggestions were legion but the consensus was that its old name was mercury (but why, I don't know) and that, in Germany, the poisonous dog's mercury Mercurialis perennis is called Bad Henry (but again, why, I don't know); so this one is called 'Good' to distinguish it. And if you either believe or understand that, you're a much better herbalist than I am. But the fact remains that this is a species that has been cultivated for centuries and it both looks and tastes rather like spinach. It's one of those plants that straddles the boundary between herbs and vegetables but since it is now a relatively uncommon plant, I shall choose to call it a herb. "

CULTIVATION AND CARE
Give a balanced general fertilizer in spring, keep well watered during the summer, cut down most of the top growth and mulch in autumn. Divide every two years.

PROBLEMS
Leaf-attacking insects, mildew, fungal leaf spots.

RECOMMENDED VARIETIES
Normal species only is available.

CICHORIUM

HERBAL INTEREST

Culinary Leaves are cooked and eaten like spinach, also young leaves fresh in salads and young flower heads like broccoli. I'm told that the young shoots make a tolerable substitute for asparagus, but have my doubts.

Non-culinary None of any great significance.

ORNAMENTAL APPEAL

About the same as spinach, which isn't very often grown for the beauty of its appearance.

SITE AND SOIL Full sun or very light shade, in rich, well fertilized and free-draining soil.

HARDINESS Very hardy, tolerating -20°C (-4°F).

SIZE Will attain about 60 x 30cm (24 x 12in) within about three years.

Chenopodium bonus-henricus

Cichorium intybus Chicory

❝ *A few years ago a good friend was very anxious that I should see his newly acquired cottage garden as it contained a most beautiful flower, one that he had never previously come across. I duly visited the rural haven to be shown a row of salad chicory with its characteristic, electric-blue daisy flowers. My friend was surprised at the identification but I had to agree with him that it was indeed a glorious thing.* ❞

HERBAL INTEREST

Culinary Flowers used in salads, roots as a vegetable or dried, roasted and ground as a coffee substitute. Roots may also be dug in autumn, kept in compost in the dark and will produce chicons, the cylindrical, blanched leafy shoots used as a slightly bitter but very tasty winter salad.

Non-culinary Various minor medicinal preparations from leaves and roots; the roots are a laxative.

CULTIVATION AND CARE

The following advice is intended for the cultivation of chicory for what I call herbal rather than mainly vegetable purposes. The plants are best grown as hardy annuals and should only be kept as perennials if they are required solely for ornamental use. Sow seed in growing positions in spring, ideally with cloche protection to give as long a growing season as possible. Mulch once plants are large

RECOMMENDED VARIETIES

It's important to select the correct variety for each purpose. If your interest is mainly ornamental, choose the normal species although if you want variation, the white- and pink-flowered forms *album* and *roseum* are available. If you want to produce chicons, then select seed of the forcing varieties, called 'Witloof' types. If you want to grow your own coffee substitute, you can make do with the 'Witloof' types or the normal species, or if you can find any, the selected variety 'Brunswick'. The rather bitter, lettuce-like vegetable, radicchio, is also a form of chichory.

ORNAMENTAL APPEAL

Rather gaunt, twiggy appearance when mature but compensated for by the superb blue flowers.

SITE AND SOIL Full sun, in rich, well fertilized and free-draining soil, preferably alkaline.

HARDINESS Hardy, tolerating about -15°C (5°F).

SIZE Will attain 1.2-1.5m x 45cm (4-5ft x 18in) by the late autumn after an early start from seed.

enough, give a balanced general fertilizer and then lift roots either for forcing or roasting when the top growth dies down in autumn.

PROBLEMS

Downy mildew, leaf-attacking insects, stem rot.

CLAYTONIA

Claytonia perfoliata Winter purslane, miner's lettuce

❝ The name 'miner's lettuce' implies that this plant is a poor relation of something better, although I must be honest and say that I find this much tastier as a winter salad plant than most of the lettuce that is sold at that time of the year. Its drawback is its smallness, for you need a lot of purslane to make a plateful. It isn't a relative of lettuce, or indeed of spinach but a member of the family that includes the ornamental alpine genus, Lewisia, *and also an equivalent summer crop,* Portulaca oleracea *(p.88), the summer purslane. You might still find it in some seed catalogues under its old name of* Montia. *❞*

ORNAMENTAL APPEAL
Not great as it looks like a weed and, to many gardeners, it probably is. Small, rounded, pale green leaves and tiny white flowers in summer on rather tall stalks.
SITE AND SOIL Full sun, in light, fairly rich but quite free-draining soil.
HARDINESS Very hardy, tolerating -20°C (-4°F) but may be damaged in cold winters.
SIZE Will attain 25-30 x 15-20cm (10-12 x 6-8in).

CULTIVATION AND CARE
Grow as a hardy annual, sowing sequentially in growing positions from spring to late summer, providing cloche protection at start of season

HERBAL INTEREST
Culinary Leaves are used as salad, especially in winter, or cooked and served as spinach.
Non-culinary None.

Claytonia perfoliata

and then through the winter. Sow in rows approximately 20cm (8in) apart and then thin the plants to 15cm (6in) within rows. Pick leaves on the cut-and-come-again principle; pull or cut away leaves as they are needed and more will grow to give further crops.

PROBLEMS
None.

RECOMMENDED VARIETIES
Normal species only is available.

Coriandrum sativum Coriander

❝ Coriander is another of those herbs that has soared in familiarity and popularity with the increased interest, in recent years, in oriental cookery. It is, nonetheless, a European species and one that has been naturalized in Britain for a very long time, although it isn't common as a wild plant. It is yet another of those white-flowered umbellifers and like so many of them, is strongly aromatic although it is an aroma that I find a bit unpleasant; something that I understood more when I discovered that its name might be derived from the Greek word for bedbug. ❞

HERBAL INTEREST
Culinary Seeds are used in curries, oriental dishes, soups, sauces, pickles, chutneys and in confectionery and pastries. Leaves are also used in soups, curries and other dishes. Stems and roots can be cooked and incorporated in dishes or served alone as a vegetable.
Non-culinary Several minor medicinal uses; sometimes used simply to disguise the taste of less pleasant medicines since it has such a strong distinctive flavour.

RECOMMENDED VARIETIES
Normal species only is available.

DIANTHUS

Coriandrum sativum

ORNAMENTAL APPEAL

Very slight for the gardener, although the contrast between the fine, feathery upper leaves and the broader, more parsley-like lower ones is rather pleasing on the eye.

SITE AND SOIL Full sun, in light, moderately rich, free-draining soil.

HARDINESS Hardy, tolerating about -15°C (5°F) but may be damaged in cold winters.

SIZE Will attain 30-50 x 25-30cm (12-20 x 10-12in).

CULTIVATION AND CARE

Grow as a hardy annual, sowing in growing positions in spring and then again in summer for overwintering under cloches. Sow in rows 20cm (8in) apart and thin plants to 15-20cm (6-8in) within rows. Pick the leaves when they are young and fresh and harvest the seeds before they are shed naturally in autumn.

PROBLEMS

None.

Dianthus spp.
Pinks

❝ *The entire notion of eating flowers is pretty alien to the British and it took an age even before nasturtiums began to appear on supermarket shelves. Gradually, however, their visual and edible appeal has become more widely appreciated; but this hasn't spread as far as the genus* Dianthus *which is still used to provide button-holes at weddings. But the petals of many varieties make interesting additions to a number of dishes. In classical times it was considered the flower of the heavens or the gods.* ❞

HERBAL INTEREST

Culinary Coloured parts of petals are used in salads, puddings, with omelettes, with meat dishes and other foods, according to scent and flavour. Also to flavour vinegar and sugar and as the flavouring of a syrup to serve with sweet dishes.

Non-culinary A few minor medicinal uses.

CULTIVATION AND CARE

Grow as short-lived perennials, giving a light dressing of balanced general fertilizer in spring but don't mulch as this tends to cause stem base rotting. Cut down dead flower heads as they fade. Take cuttings in the late summer and root in a free-draining, soil-based compost in a cold-frame. Discard the plants after about three years when they become straggly and unkempt.

Dianthus deltoides

ORNAMENTAL APPEAL

Very pretty flowers in a wide range of colours, the most attractive being the old clove-scented pinks with their frilled petals and lacy patterning.

SITE AND SOIL Full sun, in light, moderately rich, free-draining and preferably alkaline soil.

HARDINESS Very hardy, tolerating -20°C (-4°F).

SIZE Varies with type but will generally attain 30-60 x 30cm (12-24 x 12in) within three years although they don't really attain this full height as they have a flopping, sprawling habit.

RECOMMENDED VARIETIES

All the hardy outdoor *Dianthus* species may be used, including the clove-scented pinks, the maiden pinks, border carnations and the Allwoodii pinks.

PROBLEMS

Virus, leaf spots, leaf-attacking insects, thrips.

DICTAMNUS

Dictamnus albus White dittany, Burning bush

This is just one of several 'burning bushes' and it isn't the biblical one. The name is used for plants that produce a volatile and inflammable vapour that can be ignited, something that may happen spontaneously in very hot climates. This one isn't even a bush but a herbaceous perennial, superficially a bit like a low-growing delphinium although it is a relative of rue. It tends now to be grown as an ornamental border perennial but it does have a very long and varied history as a herbal plant too.

HERBAL INTEREST
Culinary Leaves are used to produce a scented tea.
Non-culinary Numerous medicinal uses, mainly as a pain-relieving treatment for such conditions as cramp, rheumatism and kidney stones.

Dictamnus albus

ORNAMENTAL APPEAL
Rather pleasing, fragrant, fresh green leaves divided into numerous oval leaflets with spikes of flowers which, despite the name, offer a choice of either white, red, pink or purple.
SITE AND SOIL Full sun or light to moderate shade, in most soils provided they are fertile and not very heavy and wet.
HARDINESS Very hardy, tolerating -20°C (-4°F).
SIZE Will attain 50-75 x 30cm (20-30 x 12in) within about three years.

CULTIVATION AND CARE
Mulch in autumn and spring, give a balanced general fertilizer in spring, cut down dead flower spikes in autumn; should not need staking. Divide every three or four years in autumn. May be propagated from seed but not all colour forms come true and are very slow to flower, so they are better increased by division.

RECOMMENDED VARIETIES
The normal species is widely available, as is *purpureus,* a variety with pink, red-veined flowers.

PROBLEMS
None.

Echium vulgare Viper's bugloss

The Boraginaceae is a most extraordinary family of plants, spanning forget-me-nots at one end and the almost tree-sized echiums of the Canary Islands and Africa at the other, with a great many rather bristly-leaved things in between. This echium is a British native but it is far from tree-sized. I don't know why it should be associated with vipers but it is one of many rather similar plants that have been found or claimed to have herbal value. While I appreciate the validity of most herbal uses, I confess to being a bit sceptical about the claim that this plant will simply 'make you less miserable'.

HERBAL INTEREST
Culinary Flowers used in salads.
Non-culinary Several minor medicinal uses for leaf extracts, including the relief of pain and fever; also seed extracts, apparently, to bring cheer.

CULTIVATION AND CARE
Sow seeds into growing position in summer, do not stake or cut down in autumn, give a light dressing of balanced general fertilizer in spring but do not mulch. Best when allowed to self-seed.

PROBLEMS
None.

RECOMMENDED VARIETIES
Normal species only is available.

EQUISETUM

ORNAMENTAL APPEAL
Tolerably attractive pink and blue flowers on a rather coarse, branched spike and elongated, oval, bristly leaves.

SITE AND SOIL Full sun, in light, free-draining, preferably alkaline soils.

HARDINESS Very hardy, tolerating -20°C (-4°F).

SIZE Will attain 75-90 x 30cm (30-34 x 12in) by the second summer of growth.

Echium vulgare

Equisetum arvense
Field horsetail

❝ *It's only with the greatest hesitation that I have included this plant because, in many another contexts, I have described it as the most ineradicable of weeds. I suppose that my advice is really to make the best of a bad thing if it grows naturally in your garden but only to consider planting it if you really are determined to have a truly comprehensive herb collection, and then only with great circumspection. If nothing else, there is always a special fascination in a spore-bearing plant that has existed in almost unaltered form for many millions of years.* ❞

HERBAL INTEREST
Culinary A rather curious-tasting tea can be made from the stems; otherwise none.

Non-culinary Used to make a wound-healing poultice for external relief.

CULTIVATION AND CARE
No attention needed, but if it is to be planted deliberately, this shoud be in a deep, lined pit as I have described for horseradish (p. 38).

PROBLEMS
None.

RECOMMENDED VARIETIES
The normal species only is available; I'm often surprised that people really do buy it.

Equisetum arvense

ORNAMENTAL APPEAL
There is a curious attraction in the Christmas-tree-like overall appearance and a fascination in the rather asparagus-like spore bearing stems.

SITE AND SOIL Full sun to light shade, will grow almost any-where but always most vigorous and invasive on any light, free-draining soils.

HARDINESS Very hardy, tolerating -20°C (-4°F).

SIZE Will attain 45-60 x 30cm (18-24 x 12in) within two years but spreads very rapidly by far-reaching rhizomes.

ERUCA

Eruca vesicaria Salad rocket, Arugula

❝ Rocket has suddenly become an 'in' plant – the thing to choose in smart restaurants and to serve at dinner parties. I wonder how many people who pay handsomely for it, however, realize that for years, it has been a waste-ground weed. This is simply a consequence of it having escaped from cottage gardens where it has been grown for centuries for its herbal value. Indeed, so widespread is it now that its true geographical origin is unknown. It is an unremarkable looking crucifer, but I have to admit that I too like its slightly tangy flavour. ❞

HERBAL INTEREST
Culinary Leaves are used to add spiciness to otherwise bland salads; can also be cooked, in the manner of almost everything else that is green and edible, 'like spinach'. The white flowers, too, are edible but unremarkable, although I once saw them used with red nasturtiums and blue chicory at a meal to mark a particularly patriotic occasion.
Non-culinary Few medicinal uses but once very important when seeds were used most extensively as the basis of a cough preparation.

CULTIVATION AND CARE
Best to sow in growing positions in succession from early spring to mid-summer, making first sowings under cloches and placing cloches on in the

ORNAMENTAL APPEAL
Minimal – rather like a small cabbage that has run to seed, or an under-fed oil seed rape.
SITE AND SOIL Full sun or light shade, in rich, well manured soil, preferably slightly alkaline although any good vegetable soil will be suitable.
HARDINESS Very hardy, tolerating -20°C (-4°F).
SIZE Will attain 60-90 x 30cm (24-34 x 12in) but only reaches full height in flower and is best picked before it reaches this.

Eruca vesicaria

autumn to give protection in winter. Space rows 12cm (5in) apart and thin to 30cm (12in) within rows. Keep well watered especially in dry periods to reduce the chance of bolting.

PROBLEMS
Flea beetles, mildew, clubroot.

Eryngium maritimum Sea holly

❝ It has taken me a long time to persuade gardeners of the value of the sea hollies (all 230 species of them) as border ornamentals, so I anticipate some difficulty in now persuading people to eat them. As far as I know, it is only the common native Eryngium maritimum *that is worth eating, but it does need the correct conditions if it is to be successful. It certainly looks like nothing else that is likely to be growing in your kitchen garden and I think the most unexpected thing about it is that it is an umbellifer. ❞*

CULTIVATION AND CARE
Mulch in spring and autumn and give a very light dressing of balanced general fertilizer in spring. Leave dead flower heads on over winter and cut old growth back in spring. Propagate by division in spring or from seed, sown in early spring under cloches, with the plants then grown as biennials.

PROBLEMS
Mildew.

EUPATORIUM

HERBAL INTEREST

Culinary Shoots with young unopened flowers and with leaves stripped off are boiled or steamed like asparagus. Young leaves may be similarly cooked.
Non-culinary Several medicinal uses, mainly with root extracts which have some healing and soothing properties.

ORNAMENTAL APPEAL

Interesting, pale bluish-green spiky, holly-like leaves with tiny flowers in bluish heads.
SITE AND SOIL Full sun, in light, free-draining, relatively nutrient-poor soil; remember that its natural habitat is on sand dunes.
HARDINESS Hardy to very hardy, tolerating -15°C (5°F) but liable to damage by any harsh, cold winter winds.
SIZE Will attain 60-75 x 30-45cm (24-30 x 12-18in) within three or four years.

Eryngium maritimum

Eupatorium purpureum Trumpet weed

❝ More hours of my school-days than I care to remember were spent, rod in hand, stalking trout along a river bank. And much of that time was spent in contact with a characteristic river-side plant called hemp agrimony, Eupatorium cannabinum, *an unexpected member of the daisy family with feathery, pinkish flower heads. This plant is its North American counterpart and I have included it almost more for sentimental reasons than anything else although it does have genuine herbal value as well. ❞*

ORNAMENTAL APPEAL

Striking, tall stems with appealing, elongated, fresh green leaves and dark reddish heads of tiny daisy-like flowers with delicate feathery heads.
SITE AND SOIL Full sun to moderate shade, in fairly rich, moist, preferably alkaline soil.
HARDINESS Very hardy, tolerating -20°C (-4°F)
SIZE Will attain 2.5-3 x 1m (8-10 x 3ft) within three or four years.

HERBAL INTEREST

Culinary None.
Non-culinary Several medicinal uses, including making from the root an extract with which to treat bladder stones.

PROBLEMS

None.

Eupatorium purpureum

CULTIVATION AND CARE

Mulch in spring and autumn and apply a balanced general fertilizer in spring. Cut back dead top growth in autumn. It may need staking on windy sites. Propagate by division in the spring or the autumn.

RECOMMENDED VARIETIES

There are several selected colour forms for ornamental use but, as a herb garden plant, the normal species is ideal.

EUPHRASIA

Euphrasia officinalis Eyebright

❝ *This one is a real challenge; but then, it's not every day that you are advised to grow a parasite in your garden. To be precise, the eyebright is a semi-parasite for it has normal green leaves for photosynthesis but is also partly parasitic on grass roots, and it is this habit that makes its cultivation a challenge. When you can grow it, however, it is a pretty thing and was once widely used in country areas for its herbal properties, hence it's common name.* **❞**

HERBAL INTEREST
Culinary None.
Non-culinary Important medicinal uses were for sore throats, allergies such as hay-fever and also as an eye treatment, although no medicament should be applied to the eyes without qualified advice.

CULTIVATION AND CARE
There are two ways of establishing eyebright and once done, it should self-seed. The first is to find a farmer with the plant growing on his grassland and ask to remove a small square of turf which can be transferred to your garden. The other option is to buy a wild flower meadow seed mixture known to include eyebright and sow this on an area of rather poor, prepared soil, which has been cleared of clay, big stones and weeds.

PROBLEMS
None.

ORNAMENTAL APPEAL
Rather pretty, with small, white and pinkish flowers on creeping, branched rather hairy stems.
SITE AND SOIL Full sun, in light, free-draining alkaline soil.
HARDINESS Very hardy, tolerating -20°C (-4°F).
SIZE Will attain about 20 x 10cm (8 x 4in) within a year but once established, individual plants are hard to distinguish within the overall mat of growth.

RECOMMENDED VARIETIES
Normal species only is available, but not widely.

Euphrasia officinalis

Filipendula ulmaria Meadowsweet

❝ *I'd grow meadowsweet in any garden, herbal or otherwise, for to me it is one of the plants most evocative of summer days, redolent with the hum of insects and a slight heat haze above the water meadow. The herbal value of meadowsweet was discovered a long time ago, and I am sure that it must always have been a plant that people noticed. What always is a surprise, nonetheless, is to know that it is a member of the rose family but perhaps the leaves are the biggest giveaway – rather like those of a large potentilla.* **❞**

HERBAL INTEREST
Culinary Flowers are used as flavouring in wines and home-made beer and in various desserts and confections.
Non-culinary Long known to have pain-relieving properties; aspirin was eventually isolated from the flower buds. It was also one of the most popular strewing herbs, used for spreading on the floor in the days before carpet.

CULTIVATION AND CARE
Mulch in spring and autumn, give a balanced general fertilizer in spring. Cut down top growth in autumn. Divide every three or four years in autumn. Propagate by division or by seed sown in spring in soil-based, humus-enriched compost in a cold-frame.

FOENICULUM

Foeniculum vulgare Fennel

❝ Fennel is one of my indispensible herbs, as much for its appearance as for its herbal value. It is a big plant, a very big plant if you consider the small amount that is needed in cooking, as its flavour is very strong. The beautiful yellow flower heads are such a welcome change from the run-of-the-mill, white umbellifers and the foliage is some of the loveliest in the entire family. ❞

HERBAL INTEREST
Culinary Seed and chopped leaves are used for aniseed flavour in fish dishes, salads, sauces and soups. Tender young stems can be chopped and also used in salads. As it is the easiest to grow of the aniseed-flavoured umbellifers, it may be used as a substitute for others.
Non-culinary Various minor medicinal uses, including an infusion from the seeds used as a treatment for constipation.

CULTIVATION AND CARE
Mulch in spring and autumn, give a balanced general fertilizer in spring. Cut down top growth in late autumn and divide every three or four years in autumn. Propagate by division or by seed sown in spring in soil-based compost in a cold-frame. Fennel self-seeds readily and many gardeners are loathe to plant it for this reason but I find it no problem provided the seedlings are pulled out promptly before the tough tap-root begins to take grip.

Foeniculum vulgare

ORNAMENTAL APPEAL
Beautiful feathery foliage in fresh, bright green or rich bronze with heads of rich yellow flowers on tall stems.
SITE AND SOIL Full sun or light shade, in fairly rich, free-draining good loam.
HARDINESS Very hardy, tolerating -20°C (-4°F).
SIZE Will attain about 1.5-2m x 60cm (5-7ft x 24in) within three or four years.

RECOMMENDED VARIETIES
Always remember that the vegetable fennel or finnocchio, with swollen stem bases is a separate variety, *dulce*. For herbal use, choose the normal species or the bronze-leaved variant, now usually called variety 'Purpureum'.

PROBLEMS
None.

Filipendula ulmaria

ORNAMENTAL APPEAL
Very pretty, feathery, cream and very fragrant (hence the name, meadowsweet) flower heads on very tall stems.
SITE AND SOIL Full sun to light or almost moderate shade, in moist, rich, fertile, preferably alkaline soil.
HARDINESS Very hardy, tolerating -20°C (-4°F).
SIZE Will attain about 1m x 45cm (3ft x 18in) within three or four years.

RECOMMENDED VARIETIES
For herb garden use, choose the normal species; the coloured-leaved and double-flowered forms are more appropriate for the herbaceous border.

PROBLEMS
None.

FRAGARIA

Fragaria vesca Wild strawberry

❝ *You may have all sorts of reasons for growing any particular plant in your herb garden but the wild strawberry will probably fit none of them. For a start it is a fruit and, you might think, merely a smaller, weedier version of the* domestic varieties. In reality, it's a fascinating plant that played a part in the ancestry of some of the cultivated forms, exceeds almost all of them in the flavour of its tiny fruit and also has herbal uses for its leaves. ❞

HERBAL INTEREST
Culinary Fruit is used as cultivated strawberries but leaves also used with cooked meat to improve flavour and as an ingredient of herbal teas.
Non-culinary Leaf tea for intestinal and urinary problems.

CULTIVATION AND CARE
May be raised from seed but best obtained as plants. If planted in a bed, space 30cm (12in) each way but I find it more attractively and appropriately planted as the edging to a herb garden. Mulch lightly in spring and autumn,

Fragaria vesca

ORNAMENTAL APPEAL
Small, white and yellow flowers in spring followed by small red fruit. Characteristic and familiar three-lobed, fresh green leaves.
SITE AND SOIL Best in light shade, in light, free-draining, preferably alkaline soil.
HARDINESS Very hardy, tolerating -20°C (-4°F).
SIZE Will attain about 25 x 25cm (10 x 10in) and spreads by runners; these may be trimmed off to keep plants more compact.

give a light dressing of a balanced fertilizer in spring and trim off foliage to a few centimetres above the crown after fruiting is finished, at the end of the summer. May be necessary to throw netting over the fruiting plants as protection from birds although I find they tend to be much more interested in the large-fruited varieties.

PROBLEMS
Slugs, mildew.

RECOMMENDED VARIETIES
Normal species only is the one to choose; the closest among cultivated varieties are the so-called Alpine strawberry types such as 'Baron Solemacher'.

Galega officinalis Goat's rue

❝ *This is another one of those species with an inexplicable name; it isn't related to the common rue as it is a member of the pea family, Leguminosae, and the association with goats seems obscure unless it has something to do with the old use of the juice in cheese-making to clot milk. Or it might just be because of its peculiar, not particularly pleasant smell. It is a big plant that won't fit into many herb gardens and is an example of those species that, I think, are better kept for a herb border where it will look rather pretty if unstartling.* ❞

HERBAL INTEREST
Culinary Juice squeezed fresh from stems will clot milk.
Non-culinary Infusions made from the dried flowers were used apparently to stimulate milk flow in nursing mothers, while seed extracts have also been used to treat diabetes, but such practices should never be carried out without medical supervision.

CULTIVATION AND CARE
Mulch in autumn and spring and give a dressing of balanced general fertilizer in spring. Cut down top growth in autumn. Propagate by division or by seed sown in spring in a soil-based compost in a cold-frame.

PROBLEMS
Mildew may be a problem if summers are hot.

GALIUM

Galium Woodruff, Bedstraw

ORNAMENTAL APPEAL
Terminal clusters of mauve, pea-like flowers with typical, much-divided, pea-like leaves.
SITE AND SOIL Full sun, in rich, fertile, preferably moist, organic soil.
HARDINESS Very hardy, tolerating -20°C (-4°F).
SIZE Will attain about 1m x 60cm (3ft x 24in) after three years.

RECOMMENDED VARIETIES
Normal species only is the one to choose although a white-flowered form, 'Alba', is also available.

Galega officinalis

❝ *Galium is a lovely genus of small, generally pretty but unspectacular and inoffensive plants, although it does include that slightly troublesome annual weed, goosegrass. There are two members well worth including in the herb garden, the sweet woodruff and the lady's bedstraw, both with* the whorls of tiny leaves so typical of the genus and heads of the most minute flowers that en masse *have a delicate, feathery appearance. The appropriately named sweet woodruff was a highly valued plant in earlier centuries, widely used as a strewing herb and in herb pillows.* ❞

Galium odoratum

ORNAMENTAL APPEAL
Pretty, small leaves in whorls with terminal masses of tiny white or yellow flowers.
SITE AND SOIL Full sun, in rich, fertile, moist but well drained soil.
HARDINESS Very hardy, tolerating -20°C (-4°F).
SIZE *G. odoratum* will attain about 30-45 x 25cm (12-18 x 10in) after two or three years; *G. verum* is a more sprawling plant but can attain double this.

CULTIVATION AND CARE
Mulch lightly in autumn and spring and give a dressing of any balanced general fertilizer in spring. Cut down top growth in autumn. Propagate by division or by seed sown fresh in late summer in soil-based compost and left to overwinter outdoors.

HERBAL INTEREST
G. odoratum Sweet Woodruff
Culinary Long known for the refreshing drink made from the dried leaves, known in Germany as the May Bowl Punch. It is generally prepared by adding sweet German or Alsace wine to the dried leaves with sugar and lemon juice and then a small quantity of brandy.
Non-culinary Several minor medicinal uses.
G. verum Lady's Bedstraw
Culinary Leaves used in cheese making to curdle milk while the flowers give it a yellow colour.
Non-culinary None.

RECOMMENDED VARIETIES
The two normal species *Galium odoratum* and *G. verum* are the only ones available.

PROBLEMS
None.

GENISTA

Genista tinctoria Dyer's greenweed

❝ *Greenweed has always struck me as a pretty unimaginative name for a plant, although the prefix 'dyer's' indicates fairly unambiguously its most important use. Yes, this native shrubby plant was once a very important source of a yellow dye and although it has no culinary herbal use and only one dubious medicinal one, I have included it because I like it and because of the decline in its use for dyeing, it is one of those native plants that is no longer as familiar as once it was.* ❞

Genista tinctoria 'Royal Gold'

HERBAL INTEREST
Culinary None.
Non-culinary Once used medicinally but now thought too toxic to be used safely.

ORNAMENTAL APPEAL
Narrowly elongated, rather dull green leaves with spikes of yellow, pea-like flowers in summer followed by pea-like pods.
SITE AND SOIL Full sun, in light, free-draining, moderately rich and preferably alkaline soil.
HARDINESS Very hardy, tolerating -20°C (-4°F).
SIZE Normal species will attain about 1.5m x 75cm (5ft x 30in) but some of the selected forms are very much lower growing than this.

RECOMMENDED VARIETIES
The normal species is widely available but there are selected ornamental forms including the double-flowered 'Flore Pleno' and 'Royal Gold' with strikingly golden flowers; both have a more procumbent habit than the normal species.

CULTIVATION AND CARE
Mulch in autumn and spring and give a dressing of balanced rose fertilizer in early spring; prune very lightly after flowering to remove old and overcrowded growth.
PROBLEMS
None.

Glycyrrhiza glabra Liquorice

❝ *Few plants are so inextricably associated with childhood and schooldays as liquorice; at least for the generation that grew up in the years immediately following the end of the Second World War. And yet how many of those who sucked liquorice sweets or even chewed the raw liquorice root that was once available (and perhaps still is), could describe the plant from which it originates. It is, in truth, a large, rather coarse although moderately attractive Mediterranean member of the pea family.* ❞

HERBAL INTEREST
Culinary Roots contain an extremely sweet-tasting substance called glycyrrhizin used to flavour confectionary and drinks.
Non-culinary Root extract is used to produce a laxative and also a preparation for coughs and throat ailments.

CULTIVATION AND CARE
Mulch in autumn and spring and give a dressing of balanced general fertilizer in the early spring; lift and divide in autumn or, in milder areas, in spring and harvest roots as needed.
PROBLEMS
None.

RECOMMENDED VARIETIES
Normal species only is usually available although there are selected culinary forms.

HELIANTHUS

ORNAMENTAL APPEAL

Rather coarse plant with large, divided leaves and narrowly elongated, generally rather sticky leaflets; upright stems of mauve or darker violet flowers.

SITE AND SOIL Full sun, in rich, preferably organic but free-draining soil.

HARDINESS Moderately hardy, tolerating about -15°C (5°F).

SIZE Will attain about 1.5m x 75cm (5ft x 30in) within about three years.

Glycyrrhiza glabra

Helianthus annuus

Helianthus annuus Sunflower

❝ *There can't be many garden plants that are as instantly familiar and generally well loved as the sunflower. It's a North American species that was cultivated there by native peoples since prehistoric times and is now grown all over the world for its spectacular growth rate and striking appearance, almost unmatched by any other half-hardy annual.* ❞

HERBAL INTEREST

Culinary The seed kernels are delicious, either on their own or in salads, and either raw or after roasting. The oil is widely used in cooking and the seeds may also be sprouted and eaten in salads. The unopened flowers may be cooked and eaten in the same manner as globe artichokes (a strange state of affairs as sunflowers are closely related to the Jerusalem artichoke).

Non-culinary Seeds and oil have been used to make preparations for the relief of gastric and kidney problems.

CULTIVATION AND CARE

Raise as a half-hardy annual; I find it best to sow directly into the growing position which should be prepared in advance by digging in plenty of well-rotted manure and compost, much as for marrows or pumpkins. Sow about two weeks before the likelihood of the last frost. To obtain sunflowers of really impressive proportions, it is essential to water regularly, apply

ORNAMENTAL APPEAL

Impressive and almost too well known to justify description: very tall leafy stems topped by massive, golden-yellow flowers of characteristic daisy form.

SITE AND SOIL Full sun with shelter from winds, in rich, preferably organic but free-draining soil.

HARDINESS Barely hardy, liking no less than -5°C (23°F).

SIZE This depends on how assiduously you water and feed; the tallest I have managed to grow 'Russian Giant' is 5.5m (17ft); but when choosing a position to sow, remember that the spread is also about 1m (3ft).

RECOMMENDED VARIETIES

There are many selected varieties of sunflower, some of them, sad to relate, dwarf. If it is to be grown as a representative of its species, however, it's my belief that if you want a sunflower, you want it big, and, in order for you to obtain a crop of seeds, it should be single rather than double flowered. 'Russian Giant' is as good a variety as you will find.

liquid fertilizer at least once a week and stake the plants, replacing the stake as the stem elongates.

PROBLEMS

Insect pests will attack the leaves but rarely cause much harm; mildew may also occur but not generally until after flowering has ceased.

HELICHRYSUM

Helichrysum italicum (syn. *H. angustifolium*) Curry plant

66 *Most of the queries that I receive about the curry plant are centred on whether such a thing really exists and, if so, does it spell less business for Indian restaurants as every one begins to make their own. The answer is, yes, it does exist, but no, it isn't the answer to homemade curry, it only smells as if it is. In any event, it comes from the wrong part of the world: southern Europe. The main garden purpose of the curry plant is to look pretty, and its striking leaves and flowers achieve this admirably. It is also sometimes suggested as a plant for edging knot gardens but I don't find that even the dwarf form is really neat enough for this purpose.* 99

ORNAMENTAL APPEAL
It has silver, needle-like leaves with heads of tiny, yellow button flowers.
SITE AND SOIL Full sun, in light, free-draining, moderately rich soil.
HARDINESS Moderately hardy, tolerating around -10°C (14°F) and may in consequence die back to soil level in cold winters.
SIZE Will attain about 45-55 x 30cm (18-22 x 12in) in two or three years.

RECOMMENDED VARIETIES
The normal species is widely available; the dwarf form is called *microphyllum* or, sometimes, 'Nanum'.

HERBAL INTEREST
Culinary Sprigs will add a mild curry flavour to dishes but it is not strong enough to substitute for the real thing.
Non-culinary None.

CULTIVATION AND CARE
Mulch in autumn and spring and give a dressing of balanced general or rose fertilizer in early spring; trim lightly in the spring to remove winter-damaged shoots and maintain a neat shape. Propagate by semi-ripe cuttings rooted in a gritty, soil-based compost in a cold-frame in summer.

PROBLEMS
None.

Helichrysum italicum

Hesperis matronalis Sweet rocket

66 *The name sweet rocket tends to be used only when this plant is grown as a herb. Wild flower gardeners and observers probably know it better as dame's violet. It is very recognisably a member of the cabbage family, Cruciferae, and looks as if it ought to have yellow, not lilac-coloured flowers. Although a native of southern Europe, it has become widely naturalized in Britain as an escape from cottage gardens where it has been grown for centuries, partly for its herbal value and partly for its flowers, at their fragrant best late in the day.* 99

HERBAL INTEREST
Culinary Leaves and flowers may be added to salads although leaves, especially, should be used with care as they have a strong flavour except when very young.
Non-culinary Minor, largely obsolete medicinal uses but was used to treat scurvy.

CULTIVATION AND CARE
Best grown as a biennial, with seeds sown in pots of soil-based compost in early summer for planting out in early autumn to flower in the following year. Will then self-seed and throw out new shoots from the base after flowering to become semi-perennial.

PROBLEMS
Mildew, caterpillars, flea beetles.

HUMULUS

Hesperis matronalis

ORNAMENTAL APPEAL
Simple, characteristically crucifer-ous flowers in shades of lilac or white, on slender stems with less characteristically cruciferous, sword-shaped leaves.
SITE AND SOIL Full sun or very light shade, in fairly rich, preferably organic, moist soil.
HARDINESS Very hardy, tolerating -20°C (-4°F).
SIZE Will attain 75cm-1m x 30cm (30in-3ft x 12in) by the second year.

RECOMMENDED VARIETIES
The normal species is widely available and probably best for herb garden use although there are also white and double-flowered forms.

Humulus lupulus Hop

" One of my odder broadcast-ing experiences concerned hops. I was required to demonstrate the traditional methods of picking and pruning hops, something that entailed balancing on wooden stilts 4m (13ft) high in the middle of a hop garden, as the commer-cial plantations are known. This illustrates that although a herba-ceous plant, a hop in full flight is mighty and should be planted with caution. "

HERBAL INTEREST
Culinary It is the dried female flower cones that are used to flavour beer but the young leaves and stems may be blanched and eaten as a vegetable or in soup.
Non-culinary The flowers are very mildly sedative and for this reason have not only been used to make tea-like infusions but are also included, dried and put in herbal pillows.

CULTIVATION AND CARE
Best grown on a screen or other free-standing support rather than against a wall. Mulch in autumn and spring and give a balanced general fertilizer in spring. No pruning needed but cut back all top growth to about 30cm (12in) above soil level in late autumn and then back to soil level in spring. Propagate by semi-ripe cuttings in late summer in a sand and peat mixture in a propagator with some bottom heat.
PROBLEMS
None.

ORNAMENTAL APPEAL
Large, coarsely toothed, rather vine-like leaves and unexpectedly dainty, cone-like female flowers.
SITE AND SOIL Full sun, with shelter from cold winds, in rich, moisture-retentive loam.
HARDINESS Moderately hardy, tolerating -15°C (5°F).
SIZE Once established, will attain 7 x 2m (22 x 7ft) within a growing season.

RECOMMENDED VARIETIES
As there is probably no differ-ence in the herbal properties, the best plant to grow is the golden-leaved variety, 'Aureus', but whether you choose this or the normal species, it is important to buy named female plants to be sure of obtaining the attractive cone-like female flowers.

Humulus lupulus

HYDRASTIS

Hydrastis canadensis Yellow root, Golden seal

This North American plant is one of the lesser known members of the buttercup family and if you are expecting beautiful, golden-yellow buttercup flowers, you will be in for a disappointment. It has a curious appeal, nonetheless, in its little greenish-white blooms that lack petals and have instead petaloid sepals. It should certainly be included in any comprehensive herb collection for it has, in the past had important medicinal uses.

RECOMMENDED VARIETIES
Normal species only is available.

CULTIVATION AND CARE
Mulch in autumn and spring and give a dressing of balanced general or rose fertilizer in the early spring. Cut back above-ground growth in late autumn. Propagate by division in autumn or from seed sown in the spring in a soil-based compost in a cold-frame.

HERBAL INTEREST
Culinary None.
Non-culinary Small amounts of the yellowish dye obtained from the roots seem to contain an antiseptic ingredient, as they have been used successfully to treat various ulcerous lesions.

ORNAMENTAL APPEAL
Rather limited; small petal-less flowers in late summer and tiny, inedible, dark red fruits on hairy stems with somewhat coarse, lobed leaves.
SITE AND SOIL Best in partial shade, in moist, but not waterlogged, rich, organic soil.
HARDINESS Very hardy, tolerating -20°C (-4°F).
SIZE Will attain about 40 x 25cm (16 x 10in) after two or three years.

PROBLEMS
None.

Hydrastis canadensis

Hypericum perforatum St John's wort

There are a great many species of Hypericum, *most of them called St John's Wort and a fair proportion of them only of moderate value as garden plants. On ornamental grounds, this very variable species would join their number but it has a number of herbal uses that justify its inclusion here. The genus as a whole is characterized by tiny dots on the leaves that can be seen when they are held up to the light. These dots are glands yielding the oil that confers the various herbal properties.*

HERBAL INTEREST
Culinary Young leaves may be added to salads to give a slightly tangy flavour.
Non-culinary Extracts from the flowers have been used to produce a treatment for bruises and similar lesions but this is now considered of rather doubtful safety.

CULTIVATION AND CARE
Mulch in the autumn and spring and give a dressing of balanced general or rose fertilizer in the early spring. Above-ground growth may be left on, in shrub fashion, but is best cut back hard in spring every second year. The best method of propagation is by the removal of naturally rooted runners in autumn or spring.

HYSSOPUS

ORNAMENTAL APPEAL
Rather limited; masses of small, star-like, yellow flowers with small, elongated, pale green leaves on a rather woody, sprawling plant.

SITE AND SOIL Full sun or light shade; tolerates most soils as long as they are not very heavy and waterlogged.

HARDINESS Very hardy, tolerating -20°C (-4°F).

SIZE Will attain 75cm-1m x 40-50cm (30in-3ft x 16-10in) after two or three years.

RECOMMENDED VARIETIES
Normal species only is available.

PROBLEMS
None.

Hypericum perforatum

Hyssopus officinalis Hyssop

❝ Hyssop is one of the best known of garden herbs. It is, like so many others, a member of the family Labiatae but not only does it have a wide range of herbal uses, it is also rather pretty in any of its variably and extensively coloured forms. It is a plant best reserved for the middle part of the herb garden, because although it is certainly good enough to be noticed, it is not quite up to genuine front-of-the-bed high standard. ❞

Hyssopus officinalis

HERBAL INTEREST
Culinary Young leaves and flowers add a spicy flavour to salads while leaves may be cooked with a wide range of meat dishes as well as being used in fruit compotes and pies.

Non-culinary Leaf infusions have been used to treat a number of internal complaints while wound-healing preparations have also been produced from the infusion of leaves.

ORNAMENTAL APPEAL
Spikes of small, labiate flowers in a range of colours on neat, rather bushy plants with massed and narrowly elongated leaves.

SITE AND SOIL Full sun, in light, free-draining, preferably alkaline soil.

HARDINESS Very hardy, tolerating -20°C (-4°F).

SIZE Will attain 75 x 30cm (30 x 12in) within each season after being cut back.

CULTIVATION AND CARE
Mulch lightly in autumn and spring and give a dressing of balanced general or rose fertilizer in early spring. Above-ground growth is best cut back hard in the spring. Propagate by the semi-ripe cuttings method in the early summer using a soil-based compost in a cold-frame.

PROBLEMS
None.

RECOMMENDED VARIETIES
The normal blue-flowered species is widely available but selected forms are offered as *albus* (white), *roseus* (pink), *purpurascens* (purple) as well as large-flowered variants.

INULA

Inula helenium Elecampane

❝ *This striking member of the Compositae is one of those herbs that could be a perfectly worthy member of the ornamental herbaceous border. Its leaves are a little large in proportion to its flowers, perhaps, but they are of a lush, fresh green colour and serve well enough their purpose of setting-off the blooms. It is now widely naturalized in Europe although it came originally from northern Asia. Oddly enough, the botanical name of this plant comprises the names of two of my favourite genera of daisies,* Inula *and* Helenium, *although it is said to derive the latter from the story that Helen of Troy was collecting the plant when she was carried off by Paris and if you believe that...* ❞

Inula helenium

HERBAL INTEREST
Culinary The root may be cooked as a vegetable but, having tried this, I cannot recommend the exercise for it has a sharp, bitter taste no matter how long it is boiled. A crystallized root extract is also eaten as a confection. It has also been used to add flavour to a number of alcoholic drinks, of which absinthe is the best known.
Non-culinary Root extract is used medicinally as an expectorant and cough relief.

ORNAMENTAL APPEAL
Large, fresh green, if slightly coarse leaves and small, rather short-rayed, golden-yellow daisy flowers in summer.
SITE AND SOIL Full sun, in rich, fairly moist but not waterlogged, loamy soil.
HARDINESS Very hardy, tolerating -20°C (-4°F) or below.
SIZE Will attain about 1-2.5m x 50cm (3-8ft x 20in) within three years, being much larger and much more lush in good growing conditions.

CULTIVATION AND CARE
Mulch in spring and autumn and give any balanced general fertilizer in autumn. Cut down above-ground growth in autumn. Is best staked in summer as it can flop rather untidily. Propagate by division in autumn.
PROBLEMS
Mildew.

RECOMMENDED VARIETIES
Normal species only is available.

Iris florentina Orris root

❝ *Iris is a huge and striking genus with a great many fine ornamental species. Surprisingly, however, it only encompasses one with herbal properties, the rather remarkable plant familiarly called* Iris florentina, *although now, more accurately,* I. 'Florentina' *for it is reckoned to be a variety derived from* I. germanica. *It is, therefore, a bearded iris, although smaller than the true species and much grown commercially, as its name suggests, in the neighbourhood of Florence. It is a notable plant in other regards too, generally being considered one of the irises that inspired the famous design of the fleur de lys of heraldry.* ❞

CULTIVATION AND CARE
In general, I find that bearded irises are best not mulched as this can encourage rotting of the surface rhizomes but they should be given a light dressing of a balanced general fertilizer or bone meal in the spring. Cut back flower stems as flowers fade and cut back foliage by about half in autumn. Does not need staking. Propagate by division of clumps after flowering. Reject the old, central area and shallowly replant the fresh young rhizomes.
PROBLEMS
Slugs and snails.

RECOMMENDED VARIETIES
Normal variety only is available.

LAMIUM

HERBAL INTEREST
Culinary None.
Non-culinary The rhizome extract has been used medicinally as a very powerful purgative and also for other minor purposes although its greatest fame arises from its use to prepare orris, a sweetly scented product used in perfumery and other cosmetics.

ORNAMENTAL APPEAL
Typical, sword-like *Iris* leaves and very pale lavender or white flowers with yellow markings in early summer.
SITE AND SOIL Full sun, in rich, but free-draining, preferably slightly alkaline soil.
HARDINESS Very hardy, tolerating -20°C (-4°F) or below.
SIZE Will attain about 75cm-1m x 30cm (30in-3ft x 12in) within three years.

Iris florentina

Lamium spp. Dead-nettles

> *It surprises me that I still have to convince some gardeners that dead-nettles have nothing to do with stinging nettles and are quite harmless. It surprises me too that I have to convince them that there are several, very attractive species and varieties within the genus, well worth growing in the ornamental border. But it surprises me most to have to persuade people that there are some that can legitimately find a home in the herb garden although, given the vast number of other herbs in the family Labiatae, this is really only to be expected.*

HERBAL INTEREST
Culinary The young leaves can be used in salads, gently steamed as a vegetable or used in soups.
Non-culinary A herbal tea may be made from dried leaves and a poultice of fresh leaves is said to have wound-healing properties.

ORNAMENTAL APPEAL
Small, toothed, heart-shaped leaves, low-growing habit and typical labiate flowers in summer.
SITE AND SOIL Full sun to moderate shade, in fairly rich, fairly free-draining soil but will flourish in most conditions.
HARDINESS Very hardy, tolerating -20°C (-4°F) or below.
SIZE Will attain about 15 x 45cm (6 x 18in) within about three years.

RECOMMENDED VARIETIES
Most of the herbal uses have been of the commonest species, *Lamium maculatum*, which exists in a wide number of varieties and among which the best are 'Beacon Silver' (richly silver foliage, pink flowers) and 'White Nancy' (silver foliage and white flowers).

Lamium maculatum 'Album'

CULTIVATION AND CARE
Mulch lightly in spring and autumn and give a balanced general fertilizer in spring. Cut down straggly, old flowering shoots towards the end of summer. Propagate by division in spring or autumn or by removal of naturally rooted runners.
PROBLEMS
Mildew.

LAVANDULA

Lavandula spp. Lavender

❝ *Many thousands of garden-ers grow lavenders in their gardens; and quite justifiably too for they are among the most evocative and (in most instances) beautifully scented of flowers that bloom in early-summer. Lavenders are versatile too, being as valuable as low, ornamental hedging as they are massed in a border or used as individual specimens in pots or other ways. Everyone must know that they have long been used in perfumery but it does surprise many to realize that they have value as culinary herbs, too.* ❞

HERBAL INTEREST
Culinary The flowers may be used in small quantities to flavour confectionary or even used in savoury dishes.
Non-culinary Lavender tea, made from the flowers, is said to be remarkably soothing and the oil has many applications in aromatherapy, in addition of course, to its use in perfumery.

CULTIVATION AND CARE
Mulch in spring and autumn and give a balanced general or rose fertilizer in spring. Trim back with shears as the flowers fade, cutting a short way into the older wood to encourage a neat habit. Propagate by semi-ripe cuttings struck in a sandy, soil-based compost in a cold-frame in summer.

PROBLEMS
None.

RECOMMENDED VARIETIES
If you are to grow a lavender in your herb garden, it should be an attractive one but the herbal, and indeed perfume value varies between the different types. The most familiar and most hardy lavenders are varieties of *Lavandula angustifolia* and include 'Alba', white flowers; 'Hidcote', rich purple flowers, neat habit, good perfume; 'Loddon Pink', taller habit, pink flowers; 'Munstead', similar to 'Hidcote' but with a rather more lax habit, slightly paler and earlier flowers; and the forms of *L. x intermedia*, which include 'Grappenhall', lavender-blue flowers, tall, rather lax habit; and 'Twickle Purple', neat compact habit, with purple flowers and soft, greyish leaves. Among other very attractive forms which are worth trying in milder gardens and sheltered spots are *L. stoechas* (French lavender), and its slightly paler flowered form *pedunculata*, with curious, whispy flowers; *L. dentata* with toothed, almost feathery leaves; and *L. viridis* with green and white flowers and bright green leaves. It must be remembered that the latter group (and several others com-monly offered for sale) *are* less hardy. Many gardeners are seduced by their alluring appear-ance and frequently end up disappointed.

ORNAMENTAL APPEAL
Familiar spikes of flowers, by no means always lavender coloured and ranging from white to very dark purple. They are appealingly set off against the generally grey-ish-green, small leaves.
SITE AND SOIL Full sun, in fairly rich, but light and very free-draining soil. Lavenders will fail miserably in the cold and wet.
HARDINESS Very hardy, tol-erating -20°C (-4°F or below) to fairly hardy, tolerating -5 to -10°C (23 to 14°F).
SIZE Varies with variety and pruning from about 45 x 30cm (18 x 12in) to 1m x 75cm (3ft x 30in) after three or four years.

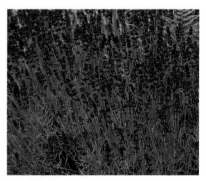

Lavandula 'Hidcote'

Lavandula angustifolia

LEVISTICUM

Lavandula stoechas pedunculata

Levisticum officinale

Levisticum officinale Lovage

❝ *It's been my experience that although many people have heard of lovage, few know what it looks like, and even fewer grow it. It is a very robust umbellifer (too robust for many gardens which accounts for its scarcity) with rather dirty-looking greenish-white flower heads and large, dark green and highly divided leaves. Its numerous herbal properties mean that it has been cultivated for centuries and although originally a Mediterranean species, it is now widely naturalized in Britain. If your herb garden is big enough, you should plant it.* ❞

RECOMMENDED VARIETIES
Normal species only is available.

HERBAL INTEREST
Culinary The young leaves may be eaten in salads, added to cooked meat dishes, used to make a most pleasing soup or made into a refreshing tea. The seeds have traditionally been added to breads and pastries but may be used to flavour savoury dishes too. Roots and young stems may be cooked as a vegetable and, although I have never tried it, I am assured that, served with a sauce, the blanched young shoots are as good as asparagus (although I've heard that said about other things too...).
Non-culinary There are various minor medicinal uses, generally for relief of kidney complaints.

CULTIVATION AND CARE
Mulch in the spring and autumn and give a balanced general fertilizer in spring. The plant may be treated

ORNAMENTAL APPEAL
The overall size and dark green leaves are the main attraction as the flowers will excite no-one.
SITE AND SOIL Full sun to light or moderate shade; will tolerate most soils, provide fairly rich and not waterlogged.
HARDINESS Very hardy, tolerating -20°C (-4°F) or below.
SIZE Will attain 2m x 75cm (7ft x 30in) within two or three years.

much as any other herbaceous perennial and cut back to soil level in the autumn although, if the stems are to be used, they are best cut young and, ideally, blanched by wrapping celery-blanching tubes around them. It is most readily propagated from seed; there will generally be self-sown seedlings available.

PROBLEMS
None.

LILIUM

Lilium candidum Madonna lily

❝ I couldn't possibly garden without lilies, which I consider head and shoulders above any other bulbs in the beauty and stateliness of their appearance. And so on purely aesthetic grounds, I'm delighted that one at least finds a place in the herb garden. The Madonna lily is, in many ways, the archetypal cottage garden lily, unusual in being one of the handful of European species, one of the relatively few that fail in acidic soils, and probably unique in its preference for shallow planting. ❞

HERBAL INTEREST
Culinary I'm told that the bulbs are cooked and eaten in parts of the eastern Mediterranean but I have never tried them.
Non-culinary An extract from the bulbs has long been used for softening hard skin, as in corns, and in ancient times, a vast number of other, generally fanciful attributes were claimed.

CULTIVATION AND CARE
Always plant with the bulbs only just covered with soil. Mulch with leaf-mould in autumn and spring and give a dressing of bone meal in early spring. Cut off dead flower heads after the blooms fade and cut back the entire plant to soil level in autumn. Like all lilies, ideally grown in pots that can be moved away as the flowers fade. Propagate by division of bulb clumps in autumn or from seed,

ORNAMENTAL APPEAL
Exquisite white, characteristically trumpet-shaped flowers in summer on rather spindly stems.
SITE AND SOIL Full sun, in light but rich and free-draining, preferably alkaline soil.
HARDINESS Very hardy, tolerating -20°C (-4°F) or below.
SIZE Will attain 1-1.5m x 25cm (3-5ft x 10in) within three years of planting a single bulb.

Lilium candidum

sown in warmth in any soil-based compost in early spring.

PROBLEMS
Botrytis, lily beetle in some areas, slugs, virus; but generally rather less prone than many lilies to the disease problems, especially virus.

RECOMMENDED VARIETIES
The normal species is the one usually seen although there is a double-flowered variant, 'Plenum'.

Linum usitatissimum Flax

❝ Every year, without fail, someone will ask me the name of the plant that is colouring a neighbouring field blue in the summer (a welcome change from the yellow rape). The answer is flax; these days, an unusual crop plant in England although it is familiar in many other areas. To be fair, the more meaningful answer would be linseed, for it is grown as an oil-seed rather than a fibre crop. Flax is an ancient plant in cultivation and has both herbal interest and a simple beauty. ❞

HERBAL INTEREST
Culinary Both seeds and the fruits used to be eaten (and may still be), apparently after being roasted, although I can only believe that the linseed oil content would inevitably make them taste like cricket bats. As the seeds are also used to prepare a laxative, the whole exercise seems fraught with danger.
Non-culinary Seeds produce a laxative and are also used to make wound-healing poultices.

CULTIVATION AND CARE
Grow as a hardy annual, either sowing seed *in situ* in spring or, if space is limited, raising a few plants in pots for planting out.

PROBLEMS
None.

LONICERA

ORNAMENTAL APPEAL

Very flimsy-looking, tall, slender stems with usually small, single, blue flowers although white and red forms exist. The individual flowers are very short-lived but are renewed daily.

SITE AND SOIL Full sun, in light but moderately rich and free-draining soil.

HARDINESS Very hardy, tolerating -20°C (-4°F) or below.

SIZE Will attain up to 1.2m x 15cm (4ft x 6in) (depending on various growing conditions) within the season.

Linum usitatissimum

RECOMMENDED VARIETIES

The normal species is the best for the herb garden although various colour selections are offered as ornamental annuals.

Lonicera caprifolium
Perfoliate honeysuckle

❝ *Honeysuckle, in the generic sense, needs no introduction. This species, however, is not the native British 'woodbine' of Shakespeare but a more southerly European species, now naturalized in parts of Britain. Having both beautiful flowers and fragrance it is perfect but perhaps too vigorous for small gardens. Most importantly here, it is the species with the most effective herbal properties.* ❞

HERBAL INTEREST

Culinary None.

Non-culinary Apart from perfumery uses, the flowers and other parts have been used to produce products ranging from laxatives to cough treatments. As the tissues contain amounts of salicylic acid, the basis of aspirin, the efficacy of these is not unexpected, but means that the plant must be employed with caution.

CULTIVATION AND CARE

Mulch in autumn and spring, preferably with leaf-mould, give a balanced rose fertilizer in spring. Cut back the oldest third of the shoots to soil level in spring and tidy up the overall structure. I always think they are best grown away from a formal house wall and discuss them in Book I of this series, *Best Climbers*. Propagated by semi-ripe cuttings in autumn in soil-based compost in a cold-frame.

PROBLEMS

Aphids, mildew.

Lonicera caprifolium

ORNAMENTAL APPEAL

Yellowish, pink-tinged flowers in summer, glaucous leaves, the uppermost united in pairs, and bright orange fruits.

SITE AND SOIL Best in light shade, and in rich, deep, organic loam.

HARDINESS Very hardy, tolerating -20°C (-4°F) or below.

SIZE Will attain 4-5m (13-16ft) in height after three or four years and will flop outwards to a considerable distance.

RECOMMENDED VARIETIES

The normal species is the one that is most suitable for the herb garden although there are one or two named variants with slightly more red-tinted flowers.

LUPINUS

Lupinus polyphyllus Lupin

❝ *Despite the fact that there is a variety of lupin named after me, I can't be enthusiastic about all of them. The more simple and clean-looking the flowers, however, the more I like them and the appropriate lupin for the herb garden is this wild, North American species from which the garden varieties are derived. The flowers in the wild plant are generally blue (although of course, a wide range of colours exists in the cultivated forms and 'Dr Stefan Buczacki' is cream).* ❞

HERBAL INTEREST
Culinary None; and should not be eaten as some parts, including the seeds, are toxic.
Non-culinary A soothing skin preparation is made from seeds.

CULTIVATION AND CARE
Mulch in autumn and spring and give a dressing of balanced general fertilizer in spring. Cut back dead flower heads as soon as the flowers fade (unless seeds are required) and cut the entire plant down to soil level as soon as mildew disfigures it. Most easily propagated from seed.
PROBLEMS
Mildew and lupin-specific aphids.

RECOMMENDED VARIETIES
The normal species is the one for the herb garden; don't be seduced by anything else, not even by me.

ORNAMENTAL APPEAL
Familiar spikes of blue, lipped flowers in early summer; the spikes are never as tall in the wild forms as the cultivated species.
SITE AND SOIL Full sun or very light shade, in light but rich and free-draining soil.
HARDINESS Very hardy, tolerating -20°C (-4°F) or below.
SIZE Will attain about 75cm-1m x 50cm (30in-3ft x 20in) after two or three years.

Lupinus polyphyllus

Malva moschata Musk mallow

❝ *There are several types of garden mallow, and several more types of plant with the epithet musk, but this particular one is unique because it combines the simply pleasing flower structure with the rich, heady musk fragrance. Several of the mallow species can be used to obtain the same herbal properties but it is this particular plant which is much the prettiest and most manageable of them, and it has the added virtue of having particularly attractive foliage.* ❞

HERBAL INTEREST
Culinary The foliage, when young, makes an unexpected and strange-looking vegetable.
Non-culinary The best known and most important of several old medicinal uses was the preparation of a cough remedy from the roots.

CULTIVATION AND CARE
Mulch in autumn and spring and give a dressing of balanced general fertilizer in spring. The plant needs careful staking for it can otherwise become an untidy mess; wrap-around supports or twiggy branches are most effective. Cut back above-ground growth in autumn. Most easily propagated from seed sown in late spring in pots of soil-based compost in a cold-frame.
PROBLEMS
Rust.

MARRUBIUM

ORNAMENTAL APPEAL

Pink or white, single, rather saucer-shaped flowers for long periods in summer, with large, finely divided, almost feathery foliage.

SITE AND SOIL Full sun or very light shade; rich and free-draining soil.

HARDINESS Very hardy, tolerating -20°C (-4°F) or below.

SIZE Will attain about 75cm-1m x 45-60cm (30in-3ft x 18-24in) after two or three years.

Malva moschata 'Alba'

RECOMMENDED VARIETIES

The normal species has pink flowers but there is definitely much to recommend the beautiful white-flowered 'Alba'.

Marrubium vulgare Horehound

" *It's fortunate that the horehound has a good herbal pedigree for it is a most unprepossessing thing that, otherwise, would be unlikely to gain garden room anywhere. It is, however, not only widespread in its distribution throughout Europe but has also been cultivated since antiquity as a cough remedy and even today, proprietary preparations include extracts of it. The unusual English name probably derives from the same source as 'hoary', meaning 'with greyish hair'.* "

CULTIVATION AND CARE

Mulch in autumn and spring, giving a dressing of balanced general fertilizer in spring. Cut down above-ground growth in autumn. Propagate by division or by seed sown in late spring in soil-based compost in a cold-frame.

PROBLEMS

None.

HERBAL INTEREST

Culinary None.

Non-culinary Cough remedies, expectorants and general cold cures are prepared from the woolly leaves.

ORNAMENTAL APPEAL

Very little, small, rather misshapen and woolly leaves with tiny white, labiate flowers in clusters on the stem in summer.

SITE AND SOIL Full sun and shelter, in a light, very free-draining soil.

HARDINESS Very hardy, tolerating -20°C (-4°F) or below.

SIZE Will attain about 45 x 25cm (18 x 10in) after two or three years.

RECOMMENDED VARIETIES

The normal species only is available.

Marrubium vulgare

MELILOTUS

Melilotus officinalis Melilot

❝ *You are more likely to find melilot in farming than gardening books as it was, in the past, an important fodder crop and has never really played a significant part in modern gardens. This is both surprising and unfortunate for it is a species with important herbal uses and, I think, a most attractive appearance. The name derives from an old word for honey, an allusion both to the plant's perfume and its value as a honey plant. I am pleased to see that it is now becoming fairly generally available at herb nurseries and I hope this will soon mean that it is more widely grown.* ❞

ORNAMENTAL APPEAL
Slender spikes of tiny, yellow, honey-scented pea flowers for long periods in summer and rather dainty, clover-like foliage.
SITE AND SOIL Full sun or very light shade, in light but fairly rich and free-draining soil.
HARDINESS Very hardy, tolerating -20°C (-4°F) or below.
SIZE Will attain about 75cm-1m x 50cm (30in-1ft x 20in) within its two year span.

CULTIVATION AND CARE
Grow as a biennial, sowing *in situ* in late spring for flowering the following year. It may also be raised in pots in a cold-frame for planting out in the following spring if space is limited.
PROBLEMS
None.

HERBAL INTEREST
Culinary Leaves are used to add flavour to stuffings. They may also be used with cheese; a related species is used in Switzerland to flavour Gruyère.
Non-culinary Various minor medicinal uses: an extract from the flowers has been used to produce an eyewash, although this should never be done without professional supervision; and leaf extracts have been used to produce an inflammation-reducing poultice.

Melilotus officinalis

RECOMMENDED VARIETIES
Normal species is the only form available.

Melissa officinalis Lemon balm

❝ *For some curious reason, a great many herbs are lemon scented; this one probably more than most. But it would find a place in any herb garden that I ever planted for another reason. In its variegated form, and in the spring, this is quite the most beautiful of all herb plants. The only real pity is that it does become a little straggly and unkempt as summer wears on. I'm unsure how long this lovely variant has been available, but there's no doubt that the herbal virtues of the species have been known since ancient times.* ❞

HERBAL INTEREST
Culinary Fresh young leaves in salads, with fish, some meat and cheese dishes and also to add lemon flavour to desserts. One of the more appealing lemon-scented teas can be made from a leaf infusion.
Non-culinary The tea is said to relieve colds and congestion while a leaf poultice has been used to aid wound healing and give relief from stings.

RECOMMENDED VARIETIES
The normal species, the lovely variegated form 'Aurea' and a less pretty golden-leaved variety 'All Gold' are all widely available.

MONARDA

Melissa officinalis 'Aurea'

ORNAMENTAL APPEAL
More or less heart-shaped, small, fresh green leaves (with a beautiful golden variegation in 'Aurea'), small, lipped, yellowish flowers in summer.
SITE AND SOIL
Full sun or very light shade, in rich, moist but not waterlogged soil.
HARDINESS
Very hardy, tolerating -20°C (-4°F) or below.
SIZE
Will attain about 75cm-1m x 50cm (30in-3ft x 20in) within three years, but this height figure is somewhat deceptive because, in the early part of the season, the plant forms a low and very neat rosette of foliage.

CULTIVATION AND CARE
Mulch lightly in autumn and spring and give a balanced general fertilizer in spring. Cut down all top growth to just above the soil level in autumn. Propagate from semi-ripe cuttings in summer; may also be successful by division if the plants aren't too old and woody.
PROBLEMS
None.

Monarda didyma Bergamot, Bee balm, Oswego tea

" *Yet another balm (the name is derived from the same source as balsam and simply means 'spicy') but although a member of the same family, Labiatae, as lemon balm, this is a very different plant and is one of those herbs that is quite as likely to be seen in the ornamental border. And while lemon balm has the fragrance of lemons, bergamot has the fragrance of oranges; I do sympathize with the Noel Coward character who complained, 'Everything smells of something else; it's dreadfully confusing'. The name 'Oswego tea' alludes to the use of the plant by the North American Oswego Indians; a use incidentally taken up by European settlers after the shortage of real tea in 1773.* "

HERBAL INTEREST
Culinary Flowers or young leaves can be used for a hint of orange in salads, added to desserts or for infusion.
Non-culinary The tea is claimed to relieve colds, congestion and similar respiratory problems and also flatulence.

CULTIVATION AND CARE
Mulch lightly in autumn and spring and give a balanced general fertilizer in spring. Cut down all top growth to just above soil level in the autumn. Propagate from semi-ripe cuttings in summer; also by division.

ORNAMENTAL APPEAL
Fresh, rather bright green, narrowly elongated leaves and heads of rather spidery, pink, purple, red or white flowers (depending on variety).
SITE AND SOIL
Full sun or light shade, in rich, moist but not waterlogged soil.
HARDINESS
Very hardy, tolerating -20°C (-4°F) or below.
SIZE
Will attain about 75cm-1m x 30cm (30in-3ft x 12in) within three years.

Monarda didyma

PROBLEMS
None.

RECOMMENDED VARIETIES
The normal species is a good herb plant but if you prefer rather more strikingly coloured flowers, then select 'Cambridge Scarlet' or even the white 'Alba'.

MENTHA

Mentha spp. Mint

❝ Mint is one of the most familiar, one of the classic, herb plants, present in almost every garden, whether or not there is a dedicated herb-growing area. Sadly, however, most gardens have but one plant, generally not of the best or most attractive variety; and that plant will have been stuck in a corner from which it has spread outwards to the point of becoming an invasive nuisance. Yes, most gardeners grow mint rather grudgingly and with little knowledge either of how to contain it or of the range of delicious colours and fragrances that the genus offers. If this book has one mission, it is to introduce more gardeners to more mints. ❞

CULTIVATION AND CARE

Over the years, I have worked out the following *modus operandi* for mint growing. I fill 20cm (8in) diameter plastic pots (with bottoms and drainage holes) with a soil-based compost (such as John Innes No.2). I then plant the mints, one per pot and sink the pots almost to the rims in the garden bed. The pots will prevent the runners from spreading into the rest of the garden. In the autumn, I lift the pots and trim off any wayward shoots that threaten to escape. Then, in every second autumn, I remove some small shoots and pot them up separately to produce fresh plants which are used to replace the old ones the following year. You will sometimes see mints for sale as seed but don't waste time with them as the best forms do not come true.

HERBAL INTEREST

Culinary Mint sauce is the best known use, together with peppermint in cool drinks and leaf sprigs with new potatoes but the delicate flavours may be used with almost any savoury or sweet dish and experimenting is fun. Infusions, especially of peppermint, produce delicious tea. For mint sauce, always scald the leaves after chopping them to release all of the flavour, and be sparing with the vinegar (use malt not wine).

Non-culinary The refreshing fragrances, either fresh or as infusions give relief, either real or imagined, from nasal congestion, headaches and other discomforts.

ORNAMENTAL APPEAL

Attractive, fresh-looking leaves, basically green but often with delightful variegations and other patterns; small purple flowers in summer.

SITE AND SOIL Full sun to light or almost moderate shade; mints are among the most shade-tolerant herbs. They tolerate most soils but will never be successful in dry and impoverished conditions.

HARDINESS Very hardy, tolerating -20°C (-4°F) or below.

SIZE Varies greatly with variety from about 1 x 10cm (½ x 4in) in two years for *M. requienni* to 1m x 60cm (3ft x 24in) for *M. longifolia*.

Mentha spicata

PROBLEMS

None.

RECOMMENDED VARIETIES

Far and away the commonest garden mint is spearmint, the mint of chewing gum, but not the best for mint sauce. So take your pick from among the following, all of which I find room for in my own, none too vast, herb garden: *Mentha* x *gracilis* 'Variegata' (ginger mint), golden-flecked leaves, gingery scent, a beauty; *M. longifolia* (horse mint), a large, coarse and unattractive plant with a spearmint scent; *M.* x *piperita* (peppermint), dark green leaves, peppermint taste, the one for summer drinks; *M. p. citrata*, (orange or eau de Cologne mint), dark bronze-green foliage and refreshing scent; *M. pulegium* (pennyroyal), small leaves, creeping habit, peppermint scent, 'Upright' is an erect growing form; *M. requienii* (Corsican mint), a tiny gem, minute leaves and flowers, creeping habit, peppermint scent, wonderful for growing in damp crevices between stones; *M. spicata* (spearmint) is the basic, standard, spearmint-scented plant – have one and use it with new potatoes, but don't use it to the exclusion of everything else. 'Crispa' is a pretty, curly leafed variant. *M. suaveolens*, (applemint), rounded, woolly leaves and apple scent, the best mint-sauce mint; *M.* x *villosa alopecuroides* ('Bowles Mint'), large, rounded hairy, apple-scented leaves, another good one for mint sauce.

Mentha x gracilis **'Variegata'**

Mentha suaveolens

Mentha suaveolens **'Variegata'**

MYOSOTIS

Myosotis spp. Forget-me-not

" *Everyone knows the forget-me-not as one of the best loved cottage-garden annuals and wild flowers. But as a herb? Surely not. Yet, in many countries, extract of both flowers and leaves has been, and indeed still is used for herbal purposes. In general, I think the perennial species have been used most, one of the main drawbacks with the annuals being that they are martyrs to mildew as the summer wears on. But any excuse to grow at least some of these delightful little blue-flowered plants as the edging to a herb garden is to be welcomed.* "

HERBAL INTEREST
Culinary None.
Non-culinary Leaf and flower extracts are used to treat lung complaints (remember that *Myosotis* is closely related to *Pulmonaria*, lungwort).

Myosotis sylvatica

ORNAMENTAL APPEAL
Small, narrowly elongated leaves and masses of familiar tiny bright blue flowers.
SITE AND SOIL Full sun or light shade; tolerates most soils if not too dry but ideally, light but fairly rich and free-draining.
HARDINESS Very hardy, tolerating -20°C (-4°F) or below.
SIZE Varies with species but annuals will attain about 25 x 25cm (10 x 10in) within the year and perennials approximately 30 x 30cm (12 x 12in) after two or three years.

CULTIVATION AND CARE
Sow annuals *in situ* and they will then self-seed year after year. Perennials scarcely need mulching but should be given a balanced general fertilizer in the spring and cut back to soil level as soon as mildew takes over in the latter part of the summer. Propagate perennials by seed sown in late spring *in situ* or by division.
PROBLEMS
Mildew.

RECOMMENDED VARIETIES
There are many annual and perennial species; perhaps the best of the perennials are *Myosotis sylvatica*, *M. alpestris* and *M. scorpioides*. The annual of which you are most likely to obtain seed is *M. arvensis*; but do avoid those cultivated selections with flowers in any colour other than blue.

Myrrhus odorata Sweet cicely

" *You could be forgiven for thinking that* Myrrhus *is the Biblical myrrh but you would be wrong, although the name, from an original Arabic word for an aromatic plant, clearly has the same source. And before anyone asks, I don't know who Cicely was, but I do know that this is one of the prettiest of the herb umbellifers that I grow. Its fresh green leaves are among the earliest growths to thrust upwards from the bare soil of the herb garden in early spring; and it has the advantage over many umbellifers, quite apart from its herbal uses, that it is only of a very modest height.* "

Myrrhus odorata

MYRTUS

Myrtus communis Myrtle

HERBAL INTEREST

Culinary Leaves are used in salads, with cooked vegetables, cooked meat dishes and also with desserts. Seeds can be added to salads and desserts and the roots cooked as a vegetable and served either hot or cold with a vinaigrette dressing.

Non-culinary Several minor medicinal uses, and to make a ubiquitous 'health-giving tonic'.

ORNAMENTAL APPEAL

Fresh, light green, ferny foliage and small umbels of pretty white spring flowers.

SITE AND SOIL Generally best in light shade, and in rich, moist but fairly free-draining soils.

HARDINESS Very hardy, tolerating -20°C (-4°F) or below.

SIZE Will attain around 1m x 45cm (3ft x 18in) within two or three years.

CULTIVATION AND CARE

Mulch in autumn and spring, give a balanced general fertilizer in the spring and cut back all above-ground growth to soil level as soon as the foliage dies in the late autumn. Propagate by division of the plants or from seed sown in late spring in a soil-based compost in a cold-frame.

PROBLEMS

Mildew.

RECOMMENDED VARIETIES

The normal species is the only one likely to be seen.

❝ Realizing that myrtle is not as tender as once I believed it to be has been one of the more valuable parts of my horticultural education in recent years. It is truly one of the most exquisitely aromatic plants and, in moderate shelter, will clearly thrive in many parts of Britain. It is worthy of a place on purely ornamental grounds and, in mild areas, makes a wonderful hedge. But it does have valuable and ancient herbal uses, too. ❞

HERBAL INTEREST

Culinary Sprigs can be used exactly as rosemary when roasting meat and the leaves as an ingredient of stuffing, especially with pork. The flowers may be used with fruit dishes and other desserts.

Non-culinary Several minor medicinal uses; leaf extracts have wound-healing and antiseptic properties.

RECOMMENDED VARIETIES

There are several named forms, including, inevitably, a double-flowered variant, but for the herb garden, the neater and more compact variety *tarentina* is the best, although I suspect that it is slightly more tender.

CULTIVATION AND CARE

Mulch in autumn and spring, give a balanced rose or other potash rich fertilizer. No pruning is necessary

ORNAMENTAL APPEAL

Masses of small, dark, evergreen leaves with beautiful, small, white, rather rose-like, cream-white flowers in summer.

SITE AND SOIL Full sun with shelter from cold winds; tolerates most soils provided not heavy and waterlogged. A good container plant in a fairly rich soil-based compost, such as John Innes No.3.

HARDINESS Fairly to moderately hardy, tolerating -10°C (14°F) or below.

SIZE Will attain around 1 x 1m (3 x 3ft) within four or five years.

Myrtus communis

although overgrown plants may be clipped in late spring. Propagate by semi-ripe cuttings in late summer, using a soil-based compost in a propagator with some bottom heat.

PROBLEMS

None.

NEPETA

Nepeta cataria Catmint

" *I have, only slightly fanci-fully, suggested planting catmint in your neighbour's garden as a means of attracting cats away from your own; for there's no denying that it does have a seemingly magnetic attraction for felines. You'd have to ask a feline why as, visually, it doesn't have a tremendous amount going for it, but I can tell you that it should find a place in the herb garden as it has several herbal merits and some rather more persuasive medicinal properties than many species.* "

ORNAMENTAL APPEAL
Not great, although the mass of greyish-green leaves and small, bluish-purple flowers are rather attractive during the summer – and until the cat rolls on them.
SITE AND SOIL Full sun; tolerates most soils if not too dry and not heavy and wet.
HARDINESS Very hardy, tolerating -20°C (-4°F) or below.
SIZE Will attain around 75 x 30cm (30 x 12in) after about three years.

CULTIVATION AND CARE
Mulch lightly in the autumn and early spring (this soon becomes difficult in spring because of its sprawling habit); give a balanced general fertilizer in the spring and cut the plant back to soil level in autumn.
PROBLEMS
Cats.

HERBAL INTEREST
Culinary Fresh leaves can be used when cooking meat, especially lamb, to add a slight mint-like flavour. Also makes a tea of tolerable taste.
Non-culinary Extracts of leaves and flowers are used to make a cold remedy, probably with some efficacy as the foliage especially has a high vitamin C content.

Nepeta cataria

RECOMMENDED VARIETIES
There are numerous species of *Nepeta*, used for a wide number of garden purposes, but the best, basic catmint is the species *N. cataria*.

Ocimum basilicum Basil

" *Basil in small pots has now become such an accepted compo-nent of supermarket herb counters that fewer gardeners are growing it fresh from seed. I suppose this increased availability is no bad thing, but it really is simplicity to grow yourself, and so much cheaper too. It is always grown as an annual although it can be a short-lived perennial but, as it is tender, it will only survive cold weather in a greenhouse or on a kitchen window ledge. But whether indoors or, perhaps best of all, in small terracotta pots outside, basil has such a fresh, fragrance and taste that you can't garden or cook without it.* "

HERBAL INTEREST
Culinary Fresh leaves are used with salads; they are especially effective when chopped and added with oil and vinegar to tomatoes. It is much used in Italian and Greek cooking and is a major contributor of that much-loved 'Mediterranean' flavour.
Non-culinary Some minor medicinal applications and widely used in aromatherapy.

CULTIVATION AND CARE
Sow as an annual in early spring, preferably in a propagator with some bottom heat. Occasional clipping in the summer will keep the plants neat.
PROBLEMS
None.

OENOTHERA

ORNAMENTAL APPEAL
More or less oval, green leaves (but smaller and/or coloured in some forms) and tiny white or pinkish flowers in the summer.
SITE AND SOIL Full sun; prefers fairly rich, free-draining soils but I always find it fares best in small pots of loam-based compost, such as John Innes No.2.
HARDINESS Barely hardy, tolerating no less than -5°C (23°F).
SIZE Will normally attain around 25 x 10cm (10 x 4in) within the season.

Ocimum basilicum

RECOMMENDED VARIETIES
Among several variants are *citriodorum*, with a lemon scent which seems to defeat the purpose of the unique basil flavour; *purpurascens*, with dark red-purple leaves (which looks attractive when combined with the plain green-leaved form); and *minimum*, the so-called Greek basil, with tiny leaves and a pretty, bushy habit but rather less flavour.

Oenothera biennis Evening primrose

Confession time: I've never really liked evening primroses because they just don't seem to offer enough in the way of flowers in relation to the overall size of the plant. But you can't ignore them in a herb garden, even if you do have to stay up late to appreciate the best of their blooms. Yes, they are evening plants but they aren't primroses, being in the same family as the willowherbs. All species of Oenothera *originated in the New World (although they are now naturalized in many other places too) and the native peoples of North America used them extensively. Wisely too, for the herbal properties are now known to have a sound biochemical basis.*

Oenothera biennis

HERBAL INTEREST
Culinary Roots, stems and leaves can be cooked as vegetables although don't become too excited at the prospect.
Non-culinary Much used medicinally, mainly for blood-associated conditions such as reducing the likelihood of blood clotting. Also used as a treatment for degenerative diseases, menopausal and other female conditions.

ORNAMENTAL APPEAL
Saucer-like, bright yellow flowers that tend to open late in the day atop tall stems with bright green, narrowly elongated leaves.
SITE AND SOIL Full sun, in fairly rich, free-draining soils and intolerant of wet, heavy and cold clays.
HARDINESS Very hardy, tolerating -20°C (-4°F).
SIZE Depending on growing conditions, will attain 1-2m x 45cm (3-7ft x 18in) within the two seasons.

CULTIVATION AND CARE
Grow as a biennial, sowing *in situ* in late spring. Once established, will generally self-seed fairly freely.
PROBLEMS
None.

RECOMMENDED VARIETIES
Among the numerous species, *Oenothera biennis* is the best and easiest for herbal use.

ONOBRYCHIS

Onobrychis viciifolia Sainfoin

❝ *The name* viciifolia *means 'having leaves like a Vicia'. And, as vicias are the vetches, and placed in the same family near to Onobrychis, the whole thing seems scarcely worthy of remark. This is another of those members of the pea family that appears to be of more interest from an agricultural than a horticultural standpoint, being an important fodder crop. And yet the sainfoin is a plant with a long and fascinating herbal history and it has recently been suggested, with sound evidence, unlike many such suggestions, that it is the sole remaining, unidentified plant of the group of sacred herbs referred to in an eleventh century Anglo-Saxon herbal.* ❞

ORNAMENTAL APPEAL

Spikes of rather pretty, rose-pink flowers and the familiar, much-divided foliage of vetches and so many other plants of the pea family.

SITE AND SOIL Full sun; always best in dryish, well drained but moderately rich soils.

HARDINESS Very hardy, tolerating -20°C (-4°F) or below.

SIZE Will attain around 50-75 x 30cm (20-30 x 12in) within two years.

RECOMMENDED VARIETIES

Normal species only is available.

Onobrychis viciifolia

HERBAL INTEREST

Culinary Both the young shoots and the leaves may be used in various salads.

Non-culinary Numerous minor medicinal merits were attached to this plant in earlier times but none seems to have survived to the present day.

CULTIVATION AND CARE

Give a very light dressing of bone meal in the spring; cut back above-ground growth hard in autumn. Best propagated from seed sown in spring in pots of any soil-based compost in a cold-frame.

PROBLEMS

None.

Onopordon acanthium Cotton thistle

❝ *You won't miss an* Onopordon *in the herb garden, or anywhere else for that matter for it is truly a giant among herbaceous plants, and achieves this stature within two seasons. It is a close relative of the familiar, wild, weed thistles and this species is also a native British plant and is now generally reckoned to be the source of the original thistle emblem of Scotland. It has a good enough herbal pedigree, both culinary and medicinal, but its size is an undeniable drawback to it being planted in the average herb garden.* ❞

HERBAL INTEREST

Culinary Unopened flowers may be cooked in exactly the same way as globe artichokes although they have even less edible matter and so you may be forgiven for wondering if it is worthwhile. The young stems may also be cooked and eaten.

Non-culinary Several historical, minor medicinal uses but apparently no longer used today.

CULTIVATION AND CARE

Sow seed in pots of soil-based compost in late spring and then plant out into their growing positions in the early autumn.

PROBLEMS

None.

ORIGANUM

Origanum spp. Marjoram and Oregano

ORNAMENTAL APPEAL
The overall size is impressive, as is the contrast between the rich purple of the flowers and the white woolly covering to the remainder of the plant.

SITE AND SOIL Full sun or very light shade; tolerates most soils but best in rich, fairly well drained sites.

HARDINESS Very hardy, tolerating -20°C (-4°F) or below.

SIZE Will attain around 2 x 1.2-1.5m (7 x 4-5ft) in favourable conditions.

RECOMMENDED VARIETIES
Normal species only is available.

Onopordon acanthium

There is a handful of truly indispensible herbs and these plants are among them, both for their culinary value, their visual appeal in flower and leaf, and their value as bee plants. Origanum is a big genus of predominantly Mediterranean species in the family Labiatae. Interestingly, while many of them are called marjorams, only one, the sole British native, tends to be known as oregano. They are all similar but differ to some degree in colour, habit and aroma.

HERBAL INTEREST
Culinary A very wide range of flavouring uses: the leaves are used in salads, stuffings, with cooked meat (chicken especially), fish, egg and cheese; almost any kitchen use is worth the experimentation. An infusion can be made from leaves and flowers to produced an aromatic tea.

Non-culinary The infusions, both of marjoram and oregano, have been claimed to cure virtually all ailments known to mankind.

CULTIVATION AND CARE
Mulching is scarcely practical but plants should be given a light dressing of bone meal in spring and the plants cut back hard to soil level in autumn. They should be renewed every three or four years and are best propagated by semi-ripe cuttings in late summer, rooted in any soil-based compost. Some varieties will also usefully form layers. The best forms do not come true from seed.

ORNAMENTAL APPEAL
Delicate leaves, in varying shades of green or gold; small white or purplish flowers which are very attractive to bees.

SITE AND SOIL Full sun or very light shade (the golden-leaved forms will scorch in full sun); tolerates most soils but best in rich, well drained sites.

HARDINESS Generally very hardy, tolerating -20°C (-4°F) or below, although some forms are only fairly hardy, tolerating no less than -5°C (23°F).

SIZE Varies with variety but most will attain 20-45 x 20-30cm (8-18 x 8-12in) after two years.

RECOMMENDED VARIETIES
Origanum vulgare (oregano or, sometimes, wild marjoram) is an untidy plant in its native form with white or pink flowers and a peppery fragrance and flavour; the beautiful golden-leaved form 'Aureum' with a milder flavour is the prettiest plant in the genus but other good varieties include the variegated 'Gold Tip', 'Compactum', with a neat, cushion habit and darker leaves, and 'Album', with white flowers.
O. majorana (sweet marjoram) is less hardy with white flowers.

PROBLEMS
None.

PAPAVER

Papaver spp. Poppy

" After dandelions and daisies, poppies must rank very high on the list of immediately recognisable flowers. And although the use of modern farm weedkillers means that the wild, annual, red field poppy is no longer as familiar as once it was, its extremely long-lived seeds means that it will still germinate and grow in disturbed soil, many years after the flowers were last seen. The poppy genus Papaver *includes several other species too, and although the perennials have no herbal interest, the fact that one of the annuals has some herbal or medicinal attraction can't have escaped many people. Wars have been fought over the product of the opium poppy and that must be treated with circumspection. "*

Papaver somniferum

HERBAL INTEREST

Culinary The seeds of both the field poppy and opium poppy are used in bread and confectionery. One of my fondest culinary childhood memories is of the Polish poppy seed cake that my father was highly adept at baking. The best seeds are those of the opium poppy, but it must be stressed that only the fully ripe seeds can be used; immature seeds are toxic.

Non-culinary Field poppy, none, and the only parts of the opium poppy that are not potentially dangerous are the ripe seeds. It is from the unripe seed capsule that the latex is extracted from which raw opium, morphine, codeine and heroine are obtained but the danger of experimenting with these substances cannot be over-stressed and in many countries, the growing of opium poppies is legally restricted.

RECOMMENDED VARIETIES

Papaver rhoeas (field poppy), single red flowers with black centre. Derived from it are many garden variants, most notably the Shirley poppies, with single or double flowers and a range of colours including red, pink and white, but never lilac or yellow. *P. somniferum*, (opium poppy), a southern European and Asian species with white, lilac or purple flowers, sometimes double.

Papaver rhoeas

ORNAMENTAL APPEAL

Single or double flowers in a range of colours from white to dark purple and red, depending on species and variety. The foliage is of little interest although the waxy, glaucous leaves and stem of *P. somniferum* are an excellent foil for the papery flowers.

SITE AND SOIL Full sun; always best in well drained but rather rich soils although field poppies are often found naturally on heavier sites too.

HARDINESS Very hardy, tolerating -20°C (-4°F) or below.

SIZE Will attain around 75cm-1m x 20cm (30in-3ft x 8in) within the season.

CULTIVATION AND CARE

Grow as a hardy annual, sowing seeds *in situ* in spring. Given a reasonably large area in which to grow, the singles will self-seed reliably year after year.

PROBLEMS

Aphids, powdery mildew and a downy mildew.

PELARGONIUM

Pelargonium spp. Scented pelargonium

> ❝ *I think that the confusion between pelargoniums and geraniums has probably at last been resolved. Most gardeners now know the difference: at its simplest, geraniums are hardy and pelargoniums tender. It may seem curious, therefore, that a group of pelargoniums find themselves in a book which is essentially about hardy plants. Indeed, it becomes odder when I point out that the pelargoniums that I have included are those that are generally grown as house or greenhouse plants.* ❞

ORNAMENTAL APPEAL
Generally small flowers in white, pink or shades of purple and mauve, usually very pretty and delicate foliage with varying degrees of indentation, with some variegated.

SITE AND SOIL May be grown in the open ground in full sun and in good, rich, free-draining soil but much better in pots of soil-based potting compost such as John Innes No.2.

HARDINESS Barely hardy, tolerating no less than -5°C (23°F).

SIZE Varies with species but most will attain around 30 x 25cm (12 x 10in) within the first season from a cutting, although a few are rather taller.

CULTIVATION AND CARE
Tender perennials, so bring under greenhouse or other protection in winter. Liquid feed with a fertilizer

RECOMMENDED VARIETIES
There are so many varieties with different scents and also so many varieties with a similar scent but different flowers and foliage that this selection must inevitably be limited to those of which I am most fond. The one variety that crops up frequently in catalogues and that should be avoided for herbal purposes is the sticky-leaved 'Filicifolium', which is slightly poisonous. In the following lists, I have indicated the fragrance first and then other notable features. Clearly some fragrances are more welcome in cooking than others (cedar-flavoured salads aren't to everyone's taste) but I include them for their general appeal.

'Attar of Roses', roses, pink flowers; 'Chocolate Tomentosum', peppermint, brown leaf blotches; 'Citriodorum', citrus, small lilac flowers; 'Clorinda', cedar, large, pink flowers; 'Copthorne', cedar, purple flowers; 'Fragrans', pine, tiny white flowers; 'Galway Star', lemon; 'Graveolens', lemon, the best known scented variety and the source of oil of geranium; 'Joy Lucille', peppermint, tiny white and mauve flowers; 'Lady Mary', nutmeg, lilac flowers; 'Lady Plymouth', lemon, the variegated-leaf form of 'Graveolens' almost as well known; 'Lilian Pottinger', pine, tiny white flowers and delightful soft leaves, my own favourite; 'Royal Oak', spicy, incense, mauve flowers.

HERBAL INTEREST
Culinary Flowers or leaves are used in salads and with cakes and other confectionery or, indeed, as they take your fancy. Experiment with both sweet and savoury dishes.

Non-culinary Extracted oils are much used in aromatherapy.

high in potash during the growing season, especially if in pots, and dead head regularly. Propagate by softwood cuttings in late summer or early spring; most types root with consummate ease.

PROBLEMS
Aphids, caterpillars.

Pelargonium **'Fragrans Variegatum'**

PETROSELINUM

Petroselinum crispum Parsley

" *Everyone knows parsley and many people know at least some of the legends attached to it: that when it grows well, for instance, this indicates that the lady of the house is the dominant partner. Many people know, too, that it can be fickle and very often doesn't germinate easily, and some realize that it isn't perennial and will die away after two years. There are even those who are aware that there are different forms of parsley, of quite distinct appearance and flavour. But whether you know a great deal or nothing about this plant, there is no denying its value and usefulness in the kitchen.* "

HERBAL INTEREST

Culinary A multitude of uses; it is a great pity when it is used merely as a garnish. Use chopped leaves in sauces, soups, with cold meat, fish and cheese dishes, with cooked vegetables and in salads. But never leave parsley garnish; it's too good to waste.

Non-culinary As with so many other herbs, an infusion can be made from the leaves and is said to be good for you. I can't comment on its effectiveness although it doesn't taste very pleasant. But I can vouch for the fact that eating fresh parsley will disperse the smell of onions or garlic from the breath like nothing else.

ORNAMENTAL APPEAL

Much-divided and often curled leaves; with many varieties in the darkest and most lush shade of green that you are likely to see.

SITE AND SOIL Full sun or very light shade in rich, well drained and preferably slightly alkaline soil.

HARDINESS Very hardy, tolerating -20°C (-4°F) or below.

SIZE 'Moss Curled' types will attain 15-20 x 15-20cm (6-8 x 6-8in) within the two seasons. More vigorous varieties may be as tall as 60cm (24in) (and of course, all varieties will be much taller if they are left to flower in the second season).

Petroselinum crispum 'Moss Curled'

RECOMMENDED VARIETIES

The 'Moss Curled' type of parsley masquerades under a number of names, depending on the company from which you buy it, but any parsley with 'Moss', 'Curled' or similar words in its name will be of rather neat, compact, dark green appearance with tightly curled leaves and a moderate flavour. There are also taller parsleys, some with tightly and some more loosely curled leaves; 'Afro' and 'Paramount 'are the best known of these. 'Darki' is a very dark green, very hardy variety, while there are also two quite distinctive natural variants: *neapolitanum* or Italian parsley is a more vigorous, upright plant with a very fine flavour and flat, rather than curled leaves. The variety *tuberosum* is generally called Hamburg parsley and is grown as a vegetable for its roots rather than as a flavouring herb.

CULTIVATION AND CARE

Grow as a biennial, either sowing *in situ* or in small pots in the greenhouse and then plant it out with the minimum of disturbance. Germination can be very slow and erratic and I always sow parsley thickly in rows about 25cm (10in) apart and, unless the soil is already at least neutral, add a little lime to the seed drill. Pouring boiling water over the drill is also said to be very effective in removing potential germination inhibitors but, in my experience, it will still fail in an acid soil. Parsley is also successful in pots provided the compost is not allowed to dry out totally.

PROBLEMS

Carrot fly, root aphid, virus.

POLYGONUM

Pimpinella anisum Aniseed

❝ *A great many umbelliferous herbs smell and taste of aniseed, but this one is the real thing. And yet, ironically, it is grown far less than many of the others. One reason is that it is an annual, but the other is probably that it is a southern European species and in more northerly gardens, most summers are not long and hot enough for the seeds to ripen. For it is the seeds that are the principal source of the flavour.* ❞

ORNAMENTAL APPEAL
Small, bright green, strawberry-like lower leaves with very finely divided upper ones. Tiny white summer flowers in rather loose umbels.
SITE AND SOIL Full sun or very light shade with shelter from cold winds, in rich, well drained and slightly alkaline soil.
HARDINESS Barely hardy, tolerating no less than -5°C (23°F).
SIZE Will attain around 45 x 25cm (18 x 10in) within season.

CULTIVATION AND CARE
Sow *in situ* in growing positions in spring. It is a fairly small plant and a group will probably be needed, so thin to a spacing of about 15-20cm (6-8in) each way.

PROBLEMS
None.

RECOMMENDED VARIETIES
Normal species only is available.

HERBAL INTEREST
Culinary Seeds add sweetness to confectionary, cheese, meat and pickles and flavour several alcoholic drinks. Flowers and leaves in salads, and roots can be added sparingly to flavour soups.
Non-culinary Used to relieve chest infections and increase milk production when breastfeeding.

Polygonum (syn. *Persicaria*) *bistorta* Bistort

❝ *Polygonum is a big genus, and most of its members are weeds. Many of those sold as ornamental herbaceous plants are unadventurous in flower and die down in autumn. This one does have herbal properties and so can't be excluded. It is rather less invasive than some of its kin and adaptable to shady spots.* ❞

HERBAL INTEREST
Culinary Young leaves in salads.
Non-culinary Root extract as an astringent; also used in mouthwash and for cough relief.

RECOMMENDED VARIETIES
Normal species is most appropriate for the herb garden.

CULTIVATION AND CARE
Trim back above-ground growth in autumn, although in mild areas it will form a more or less evergreen mat. To prevent it from becoming invasive, it should be lifted and divided

Polygonum bistorta 'Superba'

ORNAMENTAL APPEAL
Tiny pink flowers in dense club-like spikes in summer, narrowly triangular leaves.
SITE AND SOIL Full sun to moderate shade in fairly rich, moist and even wet soil, preferably acidic.
HARDINESS Very hardy, tolerating -20°C (-4°F).
SIZE Will attain around 1m x 30cm (3ft x 12in) within about two years.

every two or three years. Mulch, if practical, in autumn and spring and give a balanced general fertilizer in spring. Propagate by division or by removal of naturally rooted runners, or seed sown in late spring in pots of soil-based compost in a cold-frame.

PROBLEMS
None.

PORTULACA

Portulaca oleracea Summer purslane

" This is the summer counterpart to winter purslane (p.88). It is a half-hardy annual and one with a long history of cultivation in Asia. In consequence, the plant now grown in gardens is a selected form rather than the wild species which is more straggly and too thin-leaved to be of much value. The so-called kitchen garden purslane is a more succulent plant, easily mistaken for a sedum. Some coloured-leaved variants make good edging plants. "

CULTIVATION AND CARE
Grow as a half-hardy annual, sowing *in situ* in late spring with 30cm (12in) between rows and thinning to 10-15cm (4-6in) between plants.

PROBLEMS
None.

Portulaca oleracea

RECOMMENDED VARIETIES
The basic green plant seeds will be called 'Common' or 'Kitchen' purslane, with selected coloured-leaf forms as 'Golden' or 'Yellow'.

HERBAL INTEREST
Culinary Crisp, fresh leaves can be used in salads but should be eaten in moderation as large amounts may be diuretic. Also cooked in numerous oriental dishes and commonly preserved, pickled in vinegar
Non-culinary Minor medicinal uses, capitalizing on the diuretic properties.

ORNAMENTAL APPEAL
Small, more or less rounded, rather fleshy leaves on fleshy stems with tiny, yellow flowers in summer.
SITE AND SOIL Full sun or very light shade in moderately rich, well drained soil.
HARDINESS Barely hardy, tolerating no less than -5°C (23°F).
SIZE It will grow to attain about 15 x 25cm (6 x 10in) within the season.

Primula vulgaris

Primula spp. Primrose, cowslip

" There can't be a garden that wouldn't be improved by the addition of primroses and cowslips, but their presence in the herb garden needs some explanation; both species can be eaten in one form or another, and both have old, well tried medicinal uses. And the pleasure that their flowers bring to the spring garden is an added bonus. But do grow the true wild forms (bought, not collected) for the clarity and honesty of their yellow flowers have something that no brightly coloured garden primula will ever emulate. "

CULTIVATION AND CARE
Little needed once established, apart from a light dressing with a balanced general fertilizer in spring although they will benefit from some division every four or five years. Propagate by division or from seed sown on the surface of a light, soil-based compost at a temperature which does not exceed 20°C (68°F).

PROBLEMS
Leaf miners, virus, vine weevil, root rotting.

RECOMMENDED VARIETIES
Primula vulgaris is the primrose, with single, clear yellow flowers, one to each stem; *P. veris*, with nodding heads of many golden-yellow flowers, is the cowslip. Accept no substitutes.

PULMONARIA

Pulmonaria spp. Lungwort

HERBAL INTEREST
Culinary Cowslip leaves are good in salads but I find raw primrose a little bitter although I was once given them cooked as a vegetable and they were excellent; but you need plenty of primroses to make a square meal. The flowers of both have been used in jams, but again, large numbers are required and scattering a few primrose flowers in a salad is a better way to make the most of them.
Non-culinary All parts of primroses (but not, it seems, cowslips) can be used to make an infusion that brings relief from throat problems, headaches, and is generally very invigorating.

ORNAMENTAL APPEAL
Too well known to justify repeating but I should add that I find both primroses and cowslips have two, rather different appeals: one where there is space to grow them in close-planted masses and the other where they are grown as single specimens. But never be tempted to plant them in rows and ranks; they are too informal for that.
SITE AND SOIL Primroses thrive in light to almost moderate shade, in rich, even heavy, moisture-retentive soil. Cowslip are best grown in full sun, in light, free-draining, alkaline soil.
HARDINESS Very hardy, tolerating -20°C (-4°F).
SIZE Attains 10-25 x 10-15cm (4-10 x 4-6in) after two years.

Lungwort is one of those herbal remedies the use of which was based on the fact that its foliage resembles lung tissue. Personally, I don't mind whether or not this has any scientific basis for it enables me to include in the herb garden one of the most striking and dependable of spring-flowering perennials. Its one drawback, and it is a feature of all of the species, is that they can become invasive if left to their own devices. But, nonetheless, this is a small price to pay for an excellent plant.

HERBAL INTEREST
Culinary None.
Non-culinary Apart from the claimed value in the control of lung complaints, lungwort has also been recommended as a cure for diarrhoea.

Pulmonaria saccharata

ORNAMENTAL APPEAL
Small, bell-shaped flowers that open pink but soon turn to a lovely rich blue in the best forms. Other varieties have white or persistently red flowers. The leaves are attractively spotted in most types but are rough to the touch.
SITE AND SOIL Light to moderate shade, in fairly rich soil that does not dry out.
HARDINESS Very hardy, tolerating -20°C (-4°F).
SIZE Will attain 15-25 x 30-45cm (6-10 x 12-18in) after three years.

RECOMMENDED VARIETIES
The commonest and oldest species is *Pulmonaria officinalis* with good varieties in 'Cambridge Blue' and 'Blue Mist'. There are red- and also white-flowered forms too but these seem to lack the genuine charm of pulmonarias. Outside this species, there are fine varieties of *P. saccharata* and also some excellent hybrids, most notable 'Mawson's Blue'.

CULTIVATION AND CARE
Mulch in autumn after the foliage has been cut back to soil level and again in early spring. Give a balanced general fertilizer in spring. Propagate by division; the best forms do not come true from seed.
PROBLEMS
None.

RESEDA

Reseda luteola Weld

Weld is one of those plant names, like woad, that is redolent of ancient times, of hairy men in hairy cloth, of long-barrows, megaliths and shifting cultivation. Actually, weld is sometimes called woald but Reseda *is a different plant from* Isatis, *which produces the blue woad dye. There is a connection, nonetheless, in that the yellow dye from weld was once mixed with the blue of woad to produce a third dye called Saxon green. Both plants have been in use since ancient times and while* Reseda *is no spectacular thing, and I haven't in general included dye plants in the book, I like to grow it purely and simply because of the unbroken connection it offers with those ancient times and the early days of plant cultivation.*

HERBAL INTEREST
Culinary None.
Non-culinary Source of a bright yellow dye.

CULTIVATION AND CARE
Grow as a biennial, sowing seed *in situ* in late spring or early summer and thinning out plants in autumn to flower in the following year. Once established in appropriate conditions, should self-seed.

PROBLEMS
None.

RECOMMENDED VARIETIES
Normal species only is available.

ORNAMENTAL APPEAL
Modest; tall spikes of tiny, pale yellow-green summer flowers and narrowly elongated, wavy leaves.
SITE AND SOIL Full sun, best in a moderately rich and well drained soil.
HARDINESS Very hardy, tolerating -20°C (-4°F).
SIZE Will attain 75cm-1.2m x 30cm (30in-4ft x 12in) within the two seasons.

Reseda luteola

Rosmarinus officinalis

Rosmarinus officinalis Rosemary

Rosemary is among the handful of instantly recognisable herb plants, and is the one shrubby species that no herb garden should be without. Unfortunately, there is a general belief that rosemary can be left forever without any need for attention, the consequence being that gardens everywhere contain over-sized, misshapen straggly looking examples of a plant that can be so neat and compact as to form one of the loveliest of small hedges. Yes, grow rosemary, but grow her carefully.

RECOMMENDED VARIETIES
It is important to select varieties with care for they range widely in habit, vigour, flower colour and, to some extent, hardiness. All important garden forms are varieties of the Mediterranean *Rosmarinus officinalis*: *albiflorus*, white flowers; 'Benenden Blue' (also called 'Collingwood Ingram'), pale leaves, blue flowers, slightly citrus-like scent; 'Majorca Pink', pink flowers, less hardy; 'Miss Jessopp's Upright', blue flowers, erect, upright habit; 'Severn Sea' (not 'Seven Seas', which it is sometimes called), deep purple flowers, spreading habit, less hardy; 'Sissinghurst Blue', fine clear blue flowers.

RUBIA

ORNAMENTAL APPEAL

Very pretty, narrow, almost needle-like green leaves crowded on to the stems with masses of small, usually blue flowers intermingled in summer.

SITE AND SOIL Full sun; tolerant of a wide range of soils but always best on rich, well drained, slightly alkaline soil. Intolerant of heavy, wet conditions.

HARDINESS Varies with varieties from fairly hardy, tolerating -5 to -10°C (23 to 14°F), to hardy, tolerating -15°C (5°F).

SIZE Varies with variety from about 45 x 45cm (18 x 18in) to 2m x 75cm (7ft x 30in), without pruning.

HERBAL INTEREST

Culinary Indispensible; traditionally, of course, sprigs are used to garnish roasting lamb but it is good with other meats too and also chopped (together with the flowers) in salads.

Non-culinary Uses allied to pain relief and discomfort by improvement of blood circulation.

CULTIVATION AND CARE

Mulch in autumn and spring and give a balanced general or rose fertilizer in spring. May be clipped to shape, with inevitable loss of some flowers, or pruned by cutting out the oldest third of the branches every spring. Propagate by semi-ripe cuttings in a soil-based compost in a closed, warm propagator in late summer.

PROBLEMS

None.

Rubia tinctoria Madder

❝ *This more or less scrambling or climbing perennial is one of those rather few dye plants that also has value as a medicinal herb. It isn't a thing of great beauty but as it was once cultivated widely and achieved very considerable importance, it is well worthy of a spot in larger herb collections and is valuable, as much as anything, because climbing herbs are, (spare me the pleasure of the pun), rather thin on the ground.* ❞

Rubia tinctoria

HERBAL INTEREST

Culinary None.

Non-culinary In addition to the roots being the source of the madder dyes in reds and browns, also used to produce a treatment for disorders from urinary malfunction to constipation.

ORNAMENTAL APPEAL

Scrambling or climbing stems with rather pretty whorls of light green leaves and masses of tiny yellow flowers borne along the stem in summer.

SITE AND SOIL Full sun to light or almost moderate shade, in free-draining, fairly rich soils; intolerant of heavy conditions.

HARDINESS Hardy to very hardy, tolerating around -15°C (5°F).

SIZE Will attain a scrambling mass of about 1 x 1m (3 x 3ft) after two years.

CULTIVATION AND CARE

Mulch lightly in autumn and spring and cut back to just above soil level in late autumn. Give any balanced general fertilizer in spring. Propagate by semi-ripe cuttings in a soil-based compost in a cold-frame in summer, or by layering or by seed sown in the late spring in a soil-based compost in a cold-frame.

PROBLEMS

None.

RECOMMENDED VARIETIES

Normal species only is available.

RUMEX

Rumex acetosa Sorrel

“ *Sorrel soup seems now to be* de rigueur *in the diet of people who wouldn't know one end of a* Rumex *from the other. This new-found fashion for it amuses older gardeners, who think of* Rumex *as dock, and one of the most perni-cious of perennial weeds. The reality is that while sorrel can become invasive, it will never assume the troublesome level of dock and, fashionable or not, sorrel soup is palatable.* ”

Rumex acetosa

CULTIVATION AND CARE
Almost none needed once estab-lished although its growth will be improved by a little general fertilizer in spring, cutting down the foliage as it browns in the winter and dividing every three or four years. Propagate by division, by root cuttings or from seed, sown in early summer in a soil-based compost in a cold-frame.

HERBAL INTEREST
Culinary Young leaves are used in the aforementioned soup, in salads and also as the basis of a rather peculiar-looking sauce. But only use young leaves as they become very bitter with age.
Non-culinary An infusion of the leaves is used to treat ulcers and also for urinary complaints.

ORNAMENTAL APPEAL
Not a great deal because there's no denying that the plant *does* look like a small version of a dock with the same, elongated leaves and spike of minute pinkish flowers.
SITE AND SOIL Full sun or moderate shade, in almost any soil although less tolerant of heavy, wet conditions than their weed relatives.
HARDINESS Very hardy, tolerating -20°C (-4°F).
SIZE Will attain 60cm-1.2m x 30cm (24in-4ft x 12in) after two or three years.

RECOMMENDED VARIETIES
Normal species only is available although a very pretty related species, *Rumex scutatus*, the buckler leaf sorrel with small silvery leaves, with a shape reminiscent of those of the tulip tree, is sometimes offered.

PROBLEMS
Fungal leaf spots, leaf-eating insects.

Ruta graveolens Rue

“ *I would always include rue in a herb garden for it has a leaf form and, a colour that is unusual, if not unique among herb plants. It also has a very long herbal history and is widely rec-ommended for its culinary virtues and numerous medicinal properties but it is one of the very few gar-den herbs that I treat with consid-erable circumspection for it can cause unpleasant and even danger-ous symptoms in some people.* ”

HERBAL INTEREST
Culinary Leaves and seeds are used to give a bitter flavour to sauces and other food dressings, but to be used with caution.
Non-culinary An infusion of the leaves has long been recom-mended for the treatment of wounds and various other, blood-related conditions. But it should only be used under expert supervision as the leaves also have insecticidal properties and are particularly dangerous for pregnant women.

CULTIVATION AND CARE
Mulch in autumn and spring and give a balanced general fertilizer in spring. Prune hard in spring, but wait until all winter cold damage has occurred. Propagate by semi-ripe cuttings in summer in a soil-based compost in a cold-frame.

PROBLEMS
None.

SANGUISORBA

ORNAMENTAL APPEAL
Finely divided leaves, rather like those of a large maidenhair fern; rather disproportionately small, green-yellow flowers in summer.
SITE AND SOIL Full sun or light shade; best in moderately rich, well drained alkaline soil.
HARDINESS Hardy, tolerating about -15°C (5°F).
SIZE Will attain 50-75 x 30cm (20-30 x 12in) within two years.

RECOMMENDED VARIETIES
The normal species is widely available but two variants are much more attractive: 'Jackman's Blue', a more compact plant with steely-blue foliage, and 'Variegata', with yellowish-cream leaf blotches.

Ruta graveolens 'Jackman's Blue'

Sanguisorba minor Salad burnet

*Some things you never forget. And I never forget my first encounter with salad burnet (*Poterium sanguisorba *as it was in those days) when on a school botany field trip, the master insisted that I picked and tasted its leaves. 'Cucumber', I exclaimed in triumph and promptly pulled up a handful more. If I'd known then that the same plant is used to treat diarrhoea and haemorrhoids (I always thought the two conditions were mutually exclusive, but there you are), my enthusiasm might have been tempered. But piles, cucumber taste or not,* Sanguisorba *is a pretty little thing and every herb garden should have one.*

HERBAL INTEREST
Culinary In salads, sauces, soups, stews, casseroles, with cooked meats and in summer drinks; indeed anywhere that a cucumber flavour is desirable but the real thing is impractical.
Non-culinary An infusion of the leaves is recommended for the treatment of haemorrhoids and bowel problems.

CULTIVATION AND CARE
Mulch very lightly, if at all, in spring and give a light dressing of a balanced general fertilizer in spring. Best propagated from seed in late spring in a soil-based compost in a cold-frame.
PROBLEMS
None.

Sanguisorba minor

ORNAMENTAL APPEAL
Very pretty, almost fern-like, divided and toothed leaves; small globular flower heads in summer.
SITE AND SOIL Full sun; prefers light, free-draining, alkaline soil, just like that of the Derbyshire hillside where I first ate it.
HARDINESS Very hardy, tolerating -20°C (-4°F).
SIZE Will attain about 25-75 x 25cm (10-30 x 10in) within two or three years; those used to seeing it growing wild on hillsides may be surprised by these dimensions but in the wild, it is grazed by sheep.

RECOMMENDED VARIETIES
Normal species only is available.

SALVIA

Salvia spp. Sage

❝ A herb garden without sage isn't worthy of the name but it's a shame that so many have so few and that just one plant of one variety is sufficient for most people. There is probably a wider range in leaf colour among the various sages than in any other single group of herbs, and while some are less hardy, a representative group should be within the capability of almost all gardeners. And I am constantly amazed by the frequency with which I hear otherwise knowledgeable people say that the ornamental-foliaged forms aren't edible; they are, and I prove it every year. ❞

HERBAL INTEREST
Culinary Sage and onion stuffing is, of course, the best known use of sage and certainly the leaves are valuable with many kinds of cooked meat. The flavour is a little strong for them to be used raw in salads although the flowers can be used, both for flavour and visual appeal.
Non-culinary Many medicinal uses, an infusion of the leaves especially being valuable in assisting digestion.

CULTIVATION AND CARE
Mulch in autumn and spring and give a balanced general fertilizer in spring. Cut back dead flower heads as the the flowers fade and prune them hard in spring, cutting back to about 15-20cm (6-8in) above soil level.

ORNAMENTAL APPEAL
Broadly elongated leaves that individually are rather rough textured but offer a wide range of very attractive colour variants. Typically labiate, generally bluish-purple flowers are produced in the summer.
SITE AND SOIL Full sun, in light, free-draining, fairly rich alkaline soil.
HARDINESS Most forms are moderately hardy to very hardy, tolerating between -10 and -20°C (14 and -4°F), depending on the the variety.
SIZE Differs with variety from about 30-80 x 30-45cm (12-32 x 12-18in) after two or three years.

Salvia officinalis 'Tricolor'

Propagate by semi-ripe cuttings in summer, struck in a soil-based compost in a cold-frame.
PROBLEMS
None.

S. o. 'Aurea' & 'Purpurascens'

RECOMMENDED VARIETIES
The hardiest and easiest sages are all varieties of *Salvia officinalis* and, although the basic green-leaved species must be in your collection, you should also have: 'Albiflora', white flowers; a form called simply 'broad-leaved', with, oddly enough, broad leaves; 'Icterina', pale green leaves with gold variegation; 'Purpurascens', deep red-purple leaves; 'Purpurascens Variegata', extraordinarily variegated leaves, basically as in 'Purpurascens' but with large, angular areas in pink and cream-white; and 'Tricolor', pale green leaves with pink and white variegation. Related and useful species are *S. sclarea* (clary), with large toothed leaves and more striking flowers, it tends to be biennial in some gardens; *S. elegans*, (pineapple-scented sage) a less hardy, but very attractive plant with mint-like leaves and fragrance; *S. lavandulifolia* (lavender-leaved or Spanish sage), just about hardy and with interesting, narrow leaves.

SANTOLINA

Santolina ssp. Cotton lavender

" Santolinas, cotton lavenders, lavender cottons –you can choose which name you prefer – have become more familiar in recent years as ornamentals rather than herbs. But this plant has a long herb garden history, having origi-nated in the Mediterranean and then grown in Britain as an edging plant in knot and other formal gardens. I never find it is as good in this role as dwarf box, but, given the right growing conditions, this evergreen should be in all herb collections. "

HERBAL INTEREST
Culinary None.
Non-culinary Various minor medicinal uses, ranging from a treatment for internal parasites to the alleviation of jaundice.

Santolina chamaecyparissus

ORNAMENTAL APPEAL
Very pretty combination of small yellow flowers and neat, generally greyish or silver-green foliage.
SITE AND SOIL Full sun in light, free-draining, not very rich but not impoverished soil.
HARDINESS Moderately hardy to hardy, tolerating around -15°C (5°F).
SIZE Will attain 30-60 x 30cm (12-24 x 12in) after three years.

CULTIVATION AND CARE
Mulch lightly in autumn and spring and give a little general fertilizer in spring. Best and neatest when clipped in the spring after any likelihood of further winter cold damage is over. Propagate by semi-ripe cuttings in summer, struck in any soil-based compost in a cold-frame.
PROBLEMS
None.

RECOMMENDED VARIETIES
There are several species and many varieties, all equally attrac-tive. The commonest and longest in cultivation is *Santolina chamae-cyparissus* (in effect, cypress-leaved; also known as *S. incana*) with cheerful, golden-yellow button flowers. Selected forms include 'Lambrook Silver', markedly silvery leaves, and 'Lemon Queen', shorter, neater habit with paler flowers. Another common dwarf form is *nana* 'Pretty Carol'. *S. pinnata* has more markedly feathery leaves and, in the form *neapolitana*, these are silvery with particularly well coloured yellow flowers. 'Edward Bowles' and 'Sulphurea' are selected forms with especially good flower colours. The best of the rest is *S. rosmarinifolia* (with greener, rosemary-like leaves), most attractive of all in the variety 'Primrose Gem'.

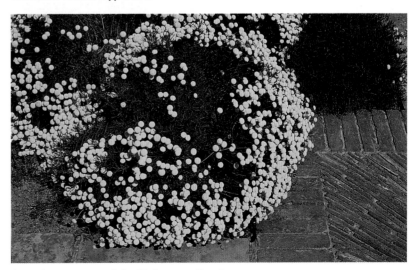

Santolina rosmarinifolia 'Primrose Gem'

SAPONARIA

Saponaria officinalis Soapwort

" *The best known soapwort in gardens today is the ornamental rock garden species,* Saponaria ocymoides, *but its cultivation history is shorter by many centuries than that of this one, the real soapwort, and the source of a real and very valuable soap. It belongs to the carnation family,* Caryophyllaceae, *as its flowers readily betray, and its soap-producing properties were known in ancient times and still find a use today, especially in the cleaning of delicate old fabrics. It is a choice herb, in its appearance, its use and its history.* "

ORNAMENTAL APPEAL
More or less oval, pointed, mid-green leaves in whorls on the stem; single pink, rather carnation-like and fragrant summer flowers.

SITE AND SOIL Full sun in light, free-draining, fairly rich alkaline soil.

HARDINESS Very hardy, tolerating -20°C (-4°F).

SIZE Will attain about 50-75 x 25cm (20-30 x 10in) after two or three years.

RECOMMENDED VARIETIES
The normal species is a fine enough plant but there are selected forms: 'Alba Plena', double white flowers; 'Rosea Plena', double pink flowers; and 'Dazzler', variegated foliage.

HERBAL INTEREST
Culinary Despite its soapy properties, the flowers may be added to salads where they impart a slightly interesting, and not remotely soap-like flavour.
Non-culinary Used to produce a skin-cleansing preparation, and a soap, extracted in boiling water.

CULTIVATION AND CARE
Mulch in autumn and spring and give a balanced general fertilizer in spring. Cut back dead flower heads as the flowers fade and cut back to just above soil level in autumn. Propagate by semi-ripe cuttings in summer, struck in a soil-based compost in a cold-frame or by removal of runners; also sown from seed, in spring in a soil-based compost in a cold-frame.

PROBLEMS
Aphids.

Saponaria officinalis

Satureja spp. Savory

" *Savory sounds as if it should be a cooking herb although the derivation of the name is different from that of savoury. There are two superficially similar species, similar in flavour but differing in that one is a shrubby perennial and the other an unexpectedly woody annual. Both have been used for many centuries, but are among those traditional and useful herbs found relatively infrequently in gardens today. Perhaps it is because they rather resemble their better known relatives, the thymes, and because people have forgotten how best to use them in the kitchen.* "

HERBAL INTEREST
Culinary Fresh leaves are used to add a peppery flavour to salads and cooked vegetables.
Non-culinary An infusion is used as an aid to digestion and also a mouth-refreshing gargle.

CULTIVATION AND CARE
Winter savory should be mulched lightly in autumn and spring and given a balanced general fertilizer in spring. Trim lightly in spring after the danger of any winter cold damage is passed. Propagate by semi-ripe cuttings in summer, struck in a soil-based compost in a cold-frame. Grow summer savory as a hardy annual, sowing *in situ* in spring.

PROBLEMS
None.

SCUTELLARIA

Satureja montana

Satureja hortensis

ORNAMENTAL APPEAL
Small, elongated dark green leaves and very small pink or white summer flowers.
SITE AND SOIL Full sun in light, free-draining, fairly rich alkaline soil.
HARDINESS Moderately hardy to hardy, tolerating around -10 to -15°C (14 to 5°F).
SIZE Both species will attain about 30-45 x 25-30cm (12-18 x 10-12in).

RECOMMENDED VARIETIES
The perennial winter savory is *Satureja montana*; the annual summer version is *S. hortensis*.

Scutellaria lateriflora Skullcap

❝ *Eating anything called skull-cap can't be an entirely enticing prospect although its ominous name relates to no more than the shape of the flowers. I don't pretend that it is an exciting species; yet another member of the huge Labiate family with some herbal properties.* Scutellaria *itself is indeed a large genus and a good many of its species have some herbal attributes. I see no point in growing more of them than is necessary, however, and so have picked this fairly widely available species as their representative.* ❞

ORNAMENTAL APPEAL
Modest; small blue, typical, lipped labiate flowers in summer on a tall, branched plant with rather coarse, toothed leaves.
SITE AND SOIL Full sun to light or almost moderate shade; tolerates most soils provided not very heavy or waterlogged.
HARDINESS Very hardy, tolerating -20°C (-4°F).
SIZE Will attain about 75cm-1m x 45cm (30in-3ft x 18in) after three years.

RECOMMENDED VARIETIES
Normal species only is available but there are related and similar forms, including the native British *Scutellaria galericulata* and *S. minor*.

HERBAL INTEREST
Culinary None.
Non-culinary Many minor medicinal uses, especially of an infusion of the leaves, used, among other things, as a treatment for hysteria.

Scutellaria lateriflora

CULTIVATION AND CARE
Mulch in autumn and spring and give a balanced general fertilizer in spring. Cut back to soil level in late autumn and divide every three or four years. Propagate by division or from semi-ripe cuttings in summer, struck in a soil-based compost in a cold-frame.

PROBLEMS
None.

SEMPERVIVUM

Sempervivum tectorum Houseleek

" *House because they grow on house roofs; leek because someone with exceptionally bad eyesight must have once thought they detected a resemblance; and* Sempervivum *because they live for a very long time and someone else must have believed that they live forever. The houseleeks must be among the most familiar of all succulents and yet it remains a surprise to many gardeners to realize that they have herbal value and, indeed, the original reason that they were cultivated (and presumably spread from gardens to roofs) was for precisely this reason. Subsequently, they were deliberately planted on houses for the fanciful belief that they would protect them from natural disasters, such as lightning.* "

ORNAMENTAL APPEAL
Striking rosettes of very fleshy, green, pink-tipped leaves. A stout spike of rich pink flowers may be produced in summer.
SITE AND SOIL It's not necessary to plant houseleeks on your roof and any site in full sun and a light free-draining, preferably slightly impoverished soil is ideal.
HARDINESS Very hardy, tolerating -20°C (-4°F).
SIZE Will attain about 8-10 x 15-20cm (3½-4 x 6-8in) after two or three years.

RECOMMENDED VARIETIES
There are numerous species of *Sempervivum* but S. *tectorum* is the original one of myth and legend.

HERBAL INTEREST
Culinary Has been used in cooking and fresh in salads but the flavour is too astringent for my liking.
Non-culinary Sap from the fresh leaves has both soothing and healing properties when applied to rashes, bites, stings and any other skin abrasions.

CULTIVATION AND CARE
Apart from a very light dressing with bonemeal in spring, none necessary. Propagate by the removal of off-sets in the spring.
PROBLEMS
None.

Sempervivum tectorum

Sesamum indicum Sesame

" *I doubt if there are many plant products so well known yet of such obscure origin as sesame seeds. There are two probable reasons for this; first, the seed can be bought so readily and thus there is no need to grow your own; and second, even though this tender plant can be grown outside in summer in Britain, the seed will only ripen in warm seasons. But that is no reason not to include it for it is strikingly different from anything else you are likely to have in your plot.* "

HERBAL INTEREST
Culinary Add the seeds to both sweet and savoury dishes to impart a delicious, rather nutty flavour and crunchy texture. In oriental cookery, the seeds are also crushed to produce a paste which is widely used.
Non-culinary Various medical benefits have been claimed for the seeds, especially associated with urinary problems.

CULTIVATION AND CARE
Raise in the same way as sweetcorn, sowing the seeds in the spring in a heated greenhouse, hardening-off the young plants and then planting them out when the danger of the last frost has passed.
PROBLEMS
None.

SIUM

Sesamum indicum

Sium sisarum
Skirret

❝ *No, skirret is the plant; a skillet is the thing in which you might cook it – a common confusion. It is an interesting herb, nonetheless, being one of the few herbal umbellifers not to have originated in Western Europe or the Mediterranean. It is an Eastern European species that was grown extensively by the Romans who took it, like so many other plants, to all corners of their empire, although it isn't known when the swollen-rooted form originated.* ❞

HERBAL INTEREST
Culinary The swollen roots are cooked and eaten in much the same way as Jerusalem artichokes. The young shoots are said also to be tasty when cooked but I have never tried them.
Non-culinary There are a number of fairly vague recommendations in herbal lore for the use of the roots and stems for the enhancement of general well being.

ORNAMENTAL APPEAL
Tall, rather cereal-like plants with broad, spreading leaves and trumpet-shaped, purplish-white flowers. The seeds are formed, in warm conditions, in elongated upright pods.
SITE AND SOIL Full sun, in a warm sheltered situation and good, rich, free-draining soils.
HARDINESS Barely hardy, tolerating no less than about -5°C (23°F).
SIZE In good conditions, will attain 1.5-2m x 75cm (5-7ft x 30in) in the season.

RECOMMENDED VARIETIES
Normal species only is available, if you are lucky and can obtain fresh seed that hasn't been killed in the drying process.

ORNAMENTAL APPEAL
Tall, and typically umbelliferous with umbels of tiny white flowers and divided leaves, less divided than those of many other species.
SITE AND SOIL Full sun or light shade; tolerates most soils but best in rich alkaline loam.
HARDINESS Very hardy, tolerating -20°C (-4°F).
SIZE Will attain 1.2-1.5m x 75cm (4-5ft x 30in) in two or three years.

CULTIVATION AND CARE
Mulch in autumn and spring and cut down the above-ground growth in autumn. Give a balanced general fertilizer in spring. Propagate by division or from seed, sown in late spring in a soil-based compost in a cold-frame.
PROBLEMS
None.

Sium sisarum

RECOMMENDED VARIETIES
The variety to grow is *sisarum* which has the swollen tuberous roots.

SMYRNIUM

Smyrnium olusatrum Alexanders

❝ *If you don't live near to the sea, you could be forgiven for not knowing that umbellifers can have yellow flowers. So many of our native species are white with feathery foliage, that coming across this naturalized one with yellow umbels and large, barely divided leaves, in its natural habitat, seldom far from the coast, is always a delightful surprise. This plant isn't named after Alexander the Great, at least not directly, for its name seems to be a reference to the city of Alexandria and an allusion, therefore, to its considerable importance to Mediterranean peoples.* ❞

HERBAL INTEREST
Culinary Many and varied uses: the young leaves in salads, the young shoots cooked as a vegetable, the roots boiled like a parsnip or Hamburg parsley, the flowers in salads, the seeds as a peppery flavouring. The seeds have even been used, ground, as a pepper substitute during times of shortage.
Non-culinary None.

CULTIVATION AND CARE
Mulch in autumn and spring and give a balanced general fertilizer in spring. Cut down above-ground growth in the autumn. Propagate by division or from seed sown in a soil-based compost in a cold-frame in early summer.
PROBLEMS
None.

ORNAMENTAL APPEAL
The combination of yellow flower heads and pale lime-green leaves is striking; indeed, I grow a similar, related but smaller species as an important ornamental biennial.
SITE AND SOIL Full sun to moderate shade in preferably fairly rich and moist but not waterlogged soil.
HARDINESS Moderately hardy, tolerating -15°C (5°F).
SIZE Will attain about 90cm-1.2m x 60cm (34in-4ft x 24in) in two years.

Smyrnium olusatrum

RECOMMENDED VARIETIES
Normal species only is available.

Stachys officinalis Betony

❝ *There are several different plants called betony, none of them strikingly attractive but all have some other interest. In the case of* Stachys officinalis, *that interest is herbal and this native British plant has long been used for a wide range of medicinal purposes. It was also used extensively in country districts as a readily available substitute for tobacco, a use that was revived during the Second World War when the real thing was hard to come by. Having no personal interest in the inflammable properties of any plant life, be it* Nicotiana *or its substitute, I cannot vouch for the taste of it.* ❞

HERBAL INTEREST
Culinary None.
Non-culinary Apart from being smoked, betony leaves have been used to make preparations with various beneficial, blood-related properties such as wound healing, as well as a migraine relief (which doesn't work for me).

CULTIVATION AND CARE
Mulch lightly in autumn and spring and give a balanced general fertilizer in spring. Cut down above-ground growth in autumn. Propagate by division or from the seed sown in a soil-based compost in a cold-frame in early summer.
PROBLEMS
None.

STELLARIA

Stachys officinalis

Stellaria media Chickweed

Surely, no gardener in his or her right mind would deliberately grow chickweed. Perhaps not although, interestingly, the presence of a good natural growth of the plant is no bad thing for it indicates a soil rich in nitrogen. And who could fail to have a soft spot for a weed that can be eaten? And seen in isolation, it is really rather a charming little thing and a small patch in a large herb garden will cause no harm and give some rather useful and not least unexpectedly appetizing vegetation.

ORNAMENTAL APPEAL
Not a great deal to become excited about: bright pink, lipped flowers on a tall stem with rather roughly toothed leaves; rather like a stretched-out dead-nettle.
SITE AND SOIL Full sun to moderate shade in preferably fairly rich and moist but not waterlogged soil.
HARDINESS Very hardy, tolerating -20°C (-4°F).
SIZE Will attain 60cm-1m x 30-45cm (24in-3ft x 12-18in) in two years.

RECOMMENDED VARIETIES
The normal species is widely available but two very predictable selected variants are 'Alba' with white flowers and 'Rosea Plena' with double pink ones.

HERBAL INTEREST
Culinary Use the plant raw in salads (I have actually seen old gardeners eating it as they weeded it from their vegetable patch). If you have sufficient, it may be lightly steamed and served as a vegetable; try it at your next smart dinner party and watch the faces when you tell them they're eating a common garden weed.
Non-culinary Used to produce a wound-treating and inflammation-reducing poultice.

CULTIVATION AND CARE
Grow as an annual, sowing the seed *in situ* and then allowing it to self-seed (try to stop it), simply pulling out excess seedlings to keep the thing within bounds.

PROBLEMS
None.

ORNAMENTAL APPEAL
Rather dainty, creeping habit, small light green leaves and very tiny white flowers.
SITE AND SOIL Full sun to light shade and almost any soil but the richer and more moist (provided not waterlogged), the better it grows.
HARDINESS Very hardy, tolerating -20°C (-4°F).
SIZE A single plant will produce a mass of growth of about 30 x 30cm (12 x 12in) within a season.

RECOMMENDED VARIETIES
The normal species is widely available; too widely available for many people's liking.

Stellaria media

SYMPHYTUM

Symphytum officinale Comfrey

❝ *Comfrey is one of those rarities: a plant that many gardeners grow with the specific intention of putting it on the compost heap. It has achieved almost divine status among the organic growing fraternity for it is generally believed to contain more nutritional value as a fertilizer than any other type of plant. It may or may not have nutritional value, but while it certainly can be eaten, it should find a place in the herb garden for its medicinal value. I am bound to say I'm pleased that comfrey does have these wonderful properties for, as a visual spectacle, it leaves a great deal to be desired.* ❞

HERBAL INTEREST
Culinary Young leaves may be used in salads or cooked as a vegetable but even when young, they are coarse and unappealing.
Non-culinary A skin preparation is made from the leaves and used to treat rashes, eczema and other irritations.

CULTIVATION AND CARE
Mulch in autumn and spring and give a balanced general fertilizer in spring. Cut down above-ground growth in autumn (or harvest leaves in bulk as needed; the plant will regenerate from the rootstock to the point of becoming invasive). Propagate by division in autumn.

PROBLEMS
None.

ORNAMENTAL APPEAL
Not very great; large, coarse bristly leaves on a large coarse plant with small, pendulous red and blue flowers. As with so many other species in the Boraginaceae, the flowers seem too small for the plant.
SITE AND SOIL Full sun, in fairly rich and moist but not waterlogged soil.
HARDINESS Very hardy, tolerating -20°C (-4°F).
SIZE Will attain 1-1.5m x 60cm (3-5ft x 24in) in two years.

Symphytum officinale

RECOMMENDED VARIETIES
The normal *Symphytum officinale* is appropriate for the herb garden although other, slightly more attractive species are also available. If your interest is in compost making, then the selected 'Bocking' strains are the ones to choose and are obtainable from specialist organic gardening suppliers.

Tagetes patula French marigold

❝ *Tagetes patula has a great deal to answer for. Firstly, it has introduced far too many gardeners to a multitude of hideously vulgar F_1 hybrid African, French and Afro-French marigolds that flood both the seed market and a great many gardens every summer. Secondly, the undoubted fact that its roots exude a secretion inhibitory to certain types of nematodes (eelworm) has also resulted in it being recommended as a cure-all for a vast range of quite unrelated garden pests and diseases. But there's no denying the wide interest in this plant and it is on these grounds, rather than for any specific herbal properties, that I include it.* ❞

ORNAMENTAL APPEAL
Pretty, finely divided, fern-like leaves and small, golden-yellow, double daisy flowers in summer.
SITE AND SOIL Full sun, in fairly rich and moist but free-draining soil.
HARDINESS Barely hardy, tolerating no less than -5°C (23°F).
SIZE Will attain 25-30cm (10-12in) within the season.

CULTIVATION AND CARE
Grow as a half-hardy annual, sowing the plants in the greenhouse in spring for hardening-off and planting out when the danger of frost has passed.

PROBLEMS
None.

TARAXACUM

HERBAL INTEREST
Culinary None.
Non-culinary No medicinal properties although a yellow dye is obtained from the flowers. The foliage, which has an acquired but I think pleasant fragrance, finds a place in pot-pourri.

RECOMMENDED VARIETIES
Grow the rather charming, small-flowered species and resist the vulgarity of the large-flowered hybrids.

Tagetes patula

Taraxacum officinale Dandelion

❝ *I'm as much a francophile as any Englishman can be; but they do surprise us sometimes. They eat horses for instance. And they also eat dandelions. Few aspects of Gallic cuisine more astonish the English than seeing dandelion leaves on the menu, but excellent they are, and just one example of the herbal versatility of this much maligned plant. And yet, few things can match the sheer spectacle of a mass of dandelion flowers in early summer, even if they are growing on your lawn.* ❞

HERBAL INTEREST
Culinary Young leaves are delicious in salads, and are even more tender if forced. Dried roots may also be ground to produce a substitute for coffee that is at least as good as chicory.
Non-culinary A number of medicinal properties are claimed: a skin treatment is prepared from the leaves and a preparation made from the roots that, *inter alia*, gives relief from constipation and insomnia (I have long wondered about the connection between the two).

CULTIVATION AND CARE
The problem is in restricting it. The best plan is as with horseradish: sink a square-sided and bottomless container in the soil and grow the plants in it, then uproot and replant from small root pieces every spring. Remove seeds to restrict spread.

Taraxacum officinale

ORNAMENTAL APPEAL
Too well known to justify detailed description; bright golden-yellow flowers and deeply toothed leaves ('dent de lion').
SITE AND SOIL Full sun to very light shade; tolerant of most soils except very acidic or very alkaline sites.
HARDINESS Very hardy, tolerating -20°C (-4°F).
SIZE Will attain from 10-30 x 10-20cm (4-12 x 4-8in) within a season, depending on the growing conditions.

RECOMMENDED VARIETIES
I have seen selected culinary strains in France, but they are not, to my knowledge, available anywhere else.

PROBLEMS
None.

TANACETUM

Tanacetum is one of those genera that has provided a home for some of the plants that botanists have tipped out of the old genus Chysanthemum, although it has collected species from other parts of the daisy family too. Many of its seventy or so members will be familiar, others much less so, but there are three that I grow in my own herb garden and which should be in yours too.

Tanacetum balsamita Alecost

❝ Even by the standards of the daisy family, the flowers of alecost are insignificant, rather like those of impoverished groundsel, but it is a plant well worth growing for its herbal value and for its long and interesting history. Attached to it is one of the most entertaining of herbal uses that I know; it is said that Puritan settlers took the plant with them to North America because chewing its leaves was a useful way of passing the hours during long and tedious sermons. The odd name 'alecost' comes, incidentally, from another old use in flavouring ale, 'cost' meaning a spicy herb. ❞

RECOMMENDED VARIETIES
The normal species is usually the only form available.

Tanacetum balsamita

HERBAL INTEREST
Culinary Young leaves may be chopped with cooked meats, in stuffings and soups to impart a slightly bitter flavour.
Non-culinary An infusion is used for colds, the relief of stings and other minor ailments and also to aid childbirth.

ORNAMENTAL APPEAL
Almost none; I have called it an impoverished groundsel and that is about all that can be said.

Tanacetum cineariifolium Pyrethrum

❝ Superficially, pyrethrum looks like almost any other single daisy, with its yellow and white flowers and finely divided leaves. But its name is familiar because the flowers have for a long time been a source of a relatively safe insecticide (which is harmless to mammals) and it is for this important reason that I include it here, for it has no direct non-culinary or culinary value. Although the extraction of the active principle isn't easy, the dried and crushed flowers themselves are a pretty reliable deterrent for crawling insects. ❞

HERBAL INTEREST
Culinary None.
Non-culinary None.

Tanacetum cineariifolium

ORNAMENTAL APPEAL

A typical single daisy with orange-centred, white-rayed flowers and finely divided, feathery leaves.

RECOMMENDED VARIETIES

The normal species only is available.

Tanacetum parthenium Feverfew

❝ As a migraine sufferer, it is one of my regrets that chewing feverfew leaves doesn't provide me with the relief that it does for many others. Nonetheless, I would always include this plant for its important herbal properties and, indeed, I would grow it even if I had no herb garden for it is a pretty plant – especially in its golden-foliaged variant – producing many daisy-like flowers in white and orange. For propagation purposes it is useful as it self-seeds slightly aggressively. ❞

RECOMMENDED VARIETIES

The normal species only is widely available but much the prettiest form is the golden-leafed 'Aureum' which comes true from seed. Double-flowered and pure white-flowered forms are also often seen under various names. As far as I know, their leaves are equally effective as a migraine treatments.

Tanacetum parthenium

HERBAL INTEREST

Culinary Leaves may be used in salads and as flavouring although they are rather bitter.

Non-culinary Use fresh leaves to reduce migraine incidence. The usual recommendation is for three or four fresh leaves daily in 'sandwiches' although I find the combination of feverfew with bread and butter revolting (almost worse than banana sandwiches) but some people find the plant causes irritation to the lips if chewed alone.

CULTIVATION AND CARE

Mulch in autumn and spring and give a balanced general fertilizer in spring. Cut down above-ground growth in autumn. Propagate by division or by seed sown *in situ* in spring (except alecost which is best sown in pots in

ORNAMENTAL APPEAL

Typical white and orange (or in some forms, all white) daisy-like flowers with neat, small, delicately divided leaves which, in the early part of the season, form an attractive rosette.

SITE AND SOIL Full sun, in light but moderately rich although well drained soil.

HARDINESS Hardy to very hardy, tolerating -15 to -20°C (5 to -4°F).

SIZE Varies with species from around 60 x 20cm (24 x 8in) after two year for feverfew to around 80 x 40cm (32 x 16in) for pyrethrum.

a soil-based compost in a cold-frame in late spring).

PROBLEMS

None.

THYMUS

Thymus spp.
Thyme

" *Thymes must be at the same time among the best known but also the least appreciated and understood of common herbs. Far too many gardeners grow inappropriate species and varieties: ornamental ones where they need culinary forms, and creeping types when what they really want is a miniature bush. But whichever of the many forms you decide is correct for you, there can be no doubt that a herb garden, indeed a garden of any sort, without some thymes, is scarcely worthy of the name. They have been grown, written and sung about, praised and used since antiquity and will be a part of gardening for as long as people garden.* "

CULTIVATION AND CARE

Little needed once fully established although best when lightly mulched in autumn and spring and given a little balanced general fertilizer in spring. Propagate by semi-ripe cuttings in late summer, rooted in a light, soil-based compost in a cold-frame. This is best done every second year and the stock plants replaced by the new plants in the following season. Thyme species may be raised from seed but unfortunately all that you will obtain are the generally straggly wild forms. The best varieties are always propagated by cuttings which are fairly easy to strike.

PROBLEMS

None.

Thymus vulgaris 'Silver Posie'

Thymus serpyllum 'Pink Chintz'

Approaching one hundred species or varieties of thyme are fairly widely obtainable and so I shall concentrate on the most important herbal types.

Thymus x *citriodorus* (lemon-scented thyme), untidy little shrub with pale pink flowers; the best forms are the coloured-leaf variants 'Golden Queen', with golden leaves, 'Silver Queen', more creeping than bushy with irregularly variegated leaves. Other common varieties such as 'Doone Valley', 'Archer's Gold' or 'Bertram Anderson' are for ornamental use.

T. herba-barona, slightly straggly, arching-creeping form with caraway flavour.

T. pseudolanuginosus, (woolly thyme), a creeping form with bright pink flowers and markedly woolly leaves.

T. pulegioides (broad-leaved thyme), a native species with larger, broader leaves and a good typical thyme flavour, but inferior I think to 'Silver Posie'.

T. serpyllum 'Pink Chintz', grey-green leaves, and small, pink flowers in clusters.

T. vulgaris, the so-called wild thyme is not a British native but a Mediterranean species and in its wild form, it is unkempt and straggly although is strongly flavoured. The best form is the neat, bush-like 'Silver Posie' with variegated leaves, to my mind, the best of all culinary varieties.

HERBAL INTEREST

Culinary Chopped leaves and flowers can be added to almost any savoury dish you wish, but they are especially good in salads and stuffings and also with cooked meats. The sweeter-flavoured forms may be used in desserts but, to my taste, there are many far better herbal sources of lemon flavour.

Non-culinary An infusion of the leaves is very refreshing and can give relief from sore throats, headaches and other similar types of ailment.

ORNAMENTAL APPEAL

Evergreen leaves in shades of green, silver or gold. Small, pink flowers but white in some forms.

SITE AND SOIL Full sun, in light but moderately rich although well drained soil; ideally neutral or slightly alkaline.

HARDINESS Hardy to very hardy, tolerating -15 to -20°C (5 to -4°F).

SIZE Varies with species from around 5 x 25cm (2 x 10in) for the smaller creeping forms to 45 x 25cm (18 x 10in) for the more vigorous bush varieties.

Thymus vulgaris

TRIGONELLA

Trigonella foenum-graecum
Fenugreek

" Far more people these days eat fenugreek than know what it is, for its sprouted seeds turn up anonymously in oriental restaurants. It has been used for centuries in a wide variety of ways and, quite apart from its herbal properties, it is extensively grown, like other members of the bean and pea family, as a fodder crop. It has a wide natural distribution in both southern Europe and Asia, which explains why it was important for peoples as distantly separated as the Greeks and the natives of southern India. As befits its origins, it is tender but, being an annual, this is no bar to its cultivation in herb gardens. "

HERBAL INTEREST
Culinary Sprouted seeds are used in and with oriental and other dishes. Larger plants cooked as a vegetable, in the manner of spinach. Roasted and ground seeds as a component of curries and other spices.
Non-culinary Crushed seeds make an unappetizing drink, said to ease flatulence, but from the taste, I'd have thought more likely to cause it.

CULTIVATION AND CARE
Grow as a half-hardy annual, sowing seed *in situ* in mid-spring in rows 20cm (8in) apart.
PROBLEMS
None.

ORNAMENTAL APPEAL
Rather slight; trifoliate, clover-like leaves and small, yellowish, pea-like flowers in summer.
SITE AND SOIL Full sun, in light but moderately rich although well drained and preferably alkaline soil.
HARDINESS Barely hardy, tolerating no less than -5°C (23°F).
SIZE A scrambling habit to produce an untidy plant 60-75cm (24-30in) tall.

RECOMMENDED VARIETIES
Normal species only is available.

Trigonella foenum-graecum

Tropaeolum majus
Nasturtium

" Thanks to the enterprise of supermarkets in including nasturtium flowers among their summer salads, these bright orange blooms must be most people's introduction to blossom eating. As readers will know by now, they are far from being the only edible flowers but there are few that are more striking, easier to grow or that make such an imposing splash of colour in the garden. "

Tropaeolum majus

CULTIVATION AND CARE
None needed once the seeds have been sown in spring and the seedlings fed until established.
PROBLEMS
Aphids and also large white butterfly caterpillars.

TUSSILAGO

HERBAL INTEREST
Culinary Flowers and flower buds can be used in salads where they add a gentle tang to the flavour and, more importantly, a vivid colour contrast to the green of other ingredients. Young seed pods can also be eaten but are rather strongly flavoured and have little visual appeal.
Non-culinary None.

ORNAMENTAL APPEAL
Unique; large, usually single flowers in vivid orange, yellow, red and cream with large rounded, dull green leaves on a vigorous scrambling plant.
SITE AND SOIL Full sun, in light and impoverished soil. In fertile conditions, flowers will be few and leaves abundant.
HARDINESS Barely hardy, tolerating no less than -5°C (23°F).
SIZE In the taller varieties produces a plant up to 3m (10ft) tall within the season.

RECOMMENDED VARIETIES
Many varieties are sold for ornamental use and, as far as I am aware, all forms are edible although I haven't tried every one. Certainly the best for garden use are the climbing and scrambling varieties such as 'Tall Mixed' and 'Giant Climbing Mixed' (the nasturtium isn't blessed with the most imaginative of names), but among others are dwarf, double-flowered and variegated forms.

Tussilago farfara
Coltsfoot

❝ One of the early shocks of my gardening life came when I was about eight years old. I had been playing my part in trying to clear a large patch of coltsfoot from a corner of our fruit garden which it had invaded from wasteland on a nearby riverbank. My surprise and consternation were considerable when I saw that very same plant for sale in a health food shop and realized that one man's meat can be another's troublesome weed. ❞

CULTIVATION AND CARE
Almost none needed, but plants should be lifted and divided every two years for they will otherwise become highly invasive. Propagate by division, from root fragments or from seed sown in pots in a soil-based compost in a cold-frame during late spring.

PROBLEMS
None.

ORNAMENTAL APPEAL
Unusually pretty although rather small, bright yellow flowers on bare, thick, scaly stems; large, more or less rounded leaves with woolly undersides emerge from the soil after the flowers.
SITE AND SOIL Full sun or light shade, in almost any soils, even those which are impoverished; also heavy sites provided they are fairly damp.
HARDINESS Very hardy, tolerating -20°C (-4°F).
SIZE Will attain approximately 30 x 45cm (12 x 18in) within two years.

HERBAL INTEREST
Culinary Young leaves can be used in salads together with chopped flowers.
Non-culinary An infusion is used for the relief of congestion and coughs.

RECOMMENDED VARIETIES
Normal species only is available.

Tussilago farfara

URTICA

Urtica dioica Stinging nettle

" *Only twenty years ago, anyone who deliberately grew stinging nettles would have been thought slightly peculiar. Then came the vogue for helping wildlife and the realization that the nettle is the food plant for some most attractive butterflies; and everyone wanted to grow a patch. Yet, if those same people had thought back thirty years, they would have realized that the nettle was much sought after in wartime, when ordinary beer was in short supply. In addition to most parts having been eaten at some time, the stems yield a strong fibre woven since the Bronze Age.* "

Urtica dioica

CULTIVATION AND CARE

Little needed once established although, as it can be invasive and is such a successful weed, it is best confined by vertical slabs in the soil; or alternatively, lifted and divided every

HERBAL INTEREST
Culinary Young leaves and shoots may be cooked as a highly nutritious and moderately tasty vegetable, and the plant can also be used as the basis of nettle beer.
Non-culinary An infusion of the young leaves produces a tonic, with rather general, allegedly 'health-giving' properties.

ORNAMENTAL APPEAL
All right if you like stinging nettles; the plant is distinctly unremarkable although I suppose the greenish, catkin-like flowers have some appeal if you can forget that the overall bristly appearance is the result of masses of highly irritant stinging hairs (the effect of which, incidentally, is lost after cooking).
SITE AND SOIL Full sun to moderate shade; will tolerate most soils but best on rich, moist loams.
HARDINESS Very hardy, tolerating -20°C (-4°F).
SIZE In good soil will attain over 1m x 30cm (3ft x 12in) within two years.

RECOMMENDED VARIETIES
Normal species only is available.

autumn. Propagate by division or from seed sown *in situ* in spring.
PROBLEMS
None.

Valeriana officinalis Valerian

" *For many years, I confused this valerian with* Centranthus, *the red valerian which has larger, more or less undivided leaves and, as far as I know, little herbal value.* Valeriana, *however, has been used for centuries and in many parts of the world for a wide range of purposes, some related to its most unusual, not to say bizarre smell.* "

ORNAMENTAL APPEAL
Heads of small, pale pink flowers on tall stems with divided leaves; pretty but not distinguished.
SITE AND SOIL Full sun to moderate shade; tolerates most soils but best on fairly rich, organic sites.
HARDINESS Very hardy, tolerating -20°C (-4°F).
SIZE Will attain approximately 1-1.5m x 50cm (3-5ft x 20in) in two or three years.

CULTIVATION AND CARE
Mulch in autumn and spring and apply a balanced general fertilizer in spring. Cut down above-ground growth in autumn. Propagate by division, although this must be performed carefully for the rootstock is easily damaged; from seed, sown in a soil-based compost in a cold-frame during spring is better.
PROBLEMS
Aphids.

VERBASCUM

Valeriana officinalis

HERBAL INTEREST

Culinary Roots may be cooked as a vegetable or used to add flavour (albeit a rather odd flavour) to cooked meat dishes, soups and stews.

Non-culinary Root extracts have been used to make a preparation that is alleged to cure everything from insomnia to exhaustion but as the same substance is also recommended to attract cats, rats and earthworms, I'm reluctant to give it a personal trial.

Verbascum thapsus Mullein

" *Mulleins are unmistakable, but, for me, also unforgivable for being biennials. Those tall, closely packed spikes of yellow flowers (and yes, mulleins should be yellow or orange, not pink as in some of the cultivated forms) really ought to last for more than two years. But they aren't plants that you can ignore and they make remarkable ornamental subjects as well as having ancient herbal value.* "

HERBAL INTEREST

Culinary None.

Non-culinary Leaves and/or flowers are used to produce remedies for migraine and respiratory problems but must be used with care and preferably under supervision because of the possible toxicity.

ORNAMENTAL APPEAL

Tall, striking flower spikes that emerge from a large rosette of distinctly woolly leaves.

SITE AND SOIL Full sun, in light, free-draining but not very rich, alkaline soil.

HARDINESS Very hardy, tolerating -20°C (-4°F).

SIZE Attains 2m x 50cm (7ft x 20in) within the two seasons.

CULTIVATION AND CARE

Grow as biennial, sowing seed in pots of soil-based compost in a cold-frame in spring and then plant out into flowering positions later in the summer.

PROBLEMS

Mildew.

RECOMMENDED VARIETIES

The normal species only is available of the native *Verbascum thapsus*. Cultivated ornamental species may lack herbal properties and be significantly toxic.

Verbascum thapsus

VERBENA

Verbena officinalis Vervain

❝ If I were to award a prize for the most pathetic flowers of any plant in the book, vervain would be on the short list. It is truly one of the most unappealing and insignificant of plants and yet it has a herbal history as long and distinguished as that of any herb. Egyptians, Greeks, Romans, Persians, and even humble Anglo-Saxons had a special place for it in their medicine and mythology. It really can't be excluded from any comprehensive herb collection and yet, ideally, it should be tucked out of sight. ❞

HERBAL INTEREST
Culinary None.
Non-culinary An infusion is used to treat sore throats, as a general sedative and, paradoxically, as an aphrodisiac.

RECOMMENDED VARIETIES
Normal species only is available.

ORNAMENTAL APPEAL
Almost non-existent; faintly chrysanthemum-like leaves and minute mauve flowers on rather spindly spikes.
SITE AND SOIL Prefers full sun to light shade; will tolerate most soils but tends to do best on loams that are rich, moist and organic.
HARDINESS Very hardy, will tolerate up to -20°C (-4°F).
SIZE Will attain 75cm-1m x 30cm (30in-3ft x 12in) within three years.

CULTIVATION AND CARE
Mulch lightly in the autumn and the spring and give a balanced general fertilizer in the spring. Cut down above-ground growth in the late autumn. Propagation is by division or alternatively from seed sown *in situ* in the spring.

PROBLEMS
None.

Verbena officinalis

Vinca major Periwinkle

❝ The periwinkles are among the most useful and valuable evergreen ground-cover plants and are especially useful in that most difficult of environments, dry shade. It comes as a surprise, albeit a pleasing one, however, to discover that they have some herbal value, too. They make ideal plants, therefore, for difficult areas in a large herb garden and, although in more confined space, the lesser species Vinca minor *would be most appropriate, it is the more robust* Vinca major *that has the better herbal pedigree. ❞*

HERBAL INTEREST
Culinary None.
Non-culinary A treatment for diabetes is prepared from the leaves although various supposedly wound-healing poultices were also once made from the plant.

CULTIVATION AND CARE
Ideally, should be mulched in autumn and spring although this is difficult once established as ground cover. Give a balanced general fertilizer in spring. Cut down above-ground growth in spring to encourage fresh new shoots. Propagate by division, by removal of natural layers from autumn to spring, or by semi-ripe cuttings in a soil-based compost in a cold-frame during summer.

PROBLEMS
Rust.

VIOLA

Vinca major

ORNAMENTAL APPEAL
Glossy, broadly elongated, ever-green leaves carried on arching, ground-covering stems with bright blue flowers.
SITE AND SOIL Full sun to moderate shade; tolerates almost all soils including dry situations.
HARDINESS Very hardy, tolerating -20°C (-4°F).
SIZE Will attain 50cm x 1m (20in x 3ft) within three years.

RECOMMENDED VARIETIES
There are many different varieties of *Vinca major* with various flower colours and leaf variegations, but rather fewer of *V. major* although 'Variegata' is an attractively variegated and rather less aggressive form while *alba* is white flowered.

Viola odorata Sweet violet

❝ *I have always admired most of what William Robinson taught us about gardening. He had a refreshingly simple approach and I have long followed his advice to use violets as a living mulch under shrub roses. The species I use is the sweet violet which will, admittedly, spread fairly effectively without any intervention on my part. I have no objection to one clump that has nudged its way into my herb garden, for the sweet violet, with its attractively perfumed, purple flowers, is as old as gardening and there is scarcely a classical writer or poet who hasn't made some allusion to its beauty and its many properties.* ❞

HERBAL INTEREST
Culinary Crystallized violets have long been used as cake decorations and a rather sickly sweet syrup may also be made from them.
Non-culinary Infusions may be prepared from flowers, leaves and roots, and are beneficial in many medicinal applications, especially the relief of head colds and congestion.

CULTIVATION AND CARE
Almost none is needed once established but a balanced general fertilizer should be given in spring. Propagate by division or by removal of naturally rooted runners.

PROBLEMS
None.

ORNAMENTAL APPEAL
A typical violet with its small, purple flowers arising from a trailing, ground-covering root-stock; it is especially welcome for appearing in the cold early months of the year.
SITE AND SOIL Prefers light to moderate shade; tolerates most soils, including dry sites, but best in rich, moist loams.
HARDINESS Very hardy, tolerating -20°C (-4°F).
SIZE Will attain 15 x 30cm (6 x 12in) within three years.

Viola odorata

RECOMMENDED VARIETIES
The normal species is the one that you will usually find although there are, as usual, double and white-flowered variants and a small group of the latter does look very pretty when inter-planted with the wild form.

HERBAL TREES AND SHRUBS

Several of the plants that I have described in the book are either more or less shrubby or are undeniably genuine shrubs. But there are also a number of ornamental shrubs and trees that have interesting or valuable herbal properties. You might like to consider their inclusion in a comprehensive herb collection or put them to use as a hedge or as a shelter belt for the protection of more tender specimens.

Buxus sempervirens Box

❝ Box is a part of our folklore, a plant that has been appreciated for centuries for its beautiful, hard, close-grained wood although it has never been a common species in Britain. Its role in the formal herb garden is an invaluable one, however, for in its slow-growing form, it is without peer as an edging and is seen at its best in the ultimate formality of knot gardens. Its growth rate, dense habit and evergreen leaves make it indispensable. ❞

Buxus sempervirens 'Suffruticosa'

FUNCTIONAL VALUE As dwarf edging or as a specimen ornamental.
ORNAMENTAL APPEAL Small, rounded, evergreen leaves, some with variegation; insignificant yellowish flowers.
SITE AND SOIL Full sun to moderate or almost deep shade; tolerates most soils but best on rich, moist and preferably alkaline loams.
HARDINESS Very hardy, tolerating -20°C (-4°F).
SIZE The more vigorous types will attain 5-6 x 5-6m (16-20 x 16-20ft) but this is of academic interest as they will be clipped to much less than this.

CULTIVATION AND CARE
Mulch in autumn and spring and give a balanced general fertilizer in spring. Clip at least twice each year, ideally in mid-summer and then again in mid-autumn. Propagate by semi-ripe cuttings in a soil-based compost in a cold-frame during summer or by hardwood cuttings in autumn.

PROBLEMS
Whitefly, box sucker, and also aphids (a box-specific species).

HERBAL INTEREST
Culinary None.
Non-culinary None.

RECOMMENDED VARIETIES
The normal species is widely obtainable and is easily the least expensive form. The variety 'Suffruticosa' is the slow-growing form to use for edging, however, and although it's often assumed that it is inherently dwarf, it will, if unpruned, eventually become rather a tall shrub. To add variety to a planting of 'Suffruticosa', odd specimens of one of the variegated types may be dotted among it: either 'Argenteovariegata', with white-margined leaves, or 'Aureovariegata' with golden leaf edges and some small blotches.

Eucalyptus spp. Gum tree

❝ I always had mixed feelings about eucalyptus. Many species are undeniably possessed of beautiful foliage and a distinctive aroma. When mature, either as individual specimens or as extensive forests, they present an imposing sight, but other than as isolated plants, I do feel they are best left in their native forests in Australia as they have a tendency to be invasive and competitive. But a small, well-contained plant of the hardy Eucalyptus globulus should find a ready welcome in the herb garden. ❞

HERBAL INTEREST
Culinary None.
Non-culinary Leaves provide oil used in cough and cold remedies and also as a treatment for burns and other skin complaints.

GAULTHERIA

FUNCTIONAL VALUE As a specimen ornamental, if given some shelter.

ORNAMENTAL APPEAL Rounded, glaucous young foliage; elongated, spearhead-shaped mature leaves; peeling, grey bark.

SITE AND SOIL Full sun with shelter from cold winds; tolerates most soils but best on rich, organic loams.

HARDINESS Fairly hardy, tolerating around -10°C (14°F).

SIZE Allowed to reach maturity in mild areas in Britain, *E. globulus* will attain 15m (50ft) after ten years and ultimately, perhaps 40m (120ft).

CULTIVATION AND CARE

Mulch in autumn and spring and give a balanced general fertilizer in spring. Prune back to within 30cm (12in) of soil level in spring to encourage a dwarf, shrubby habit with the attractive juvenile foliage. Allowed to grow tall, the tree will soon become less attractive, out of hand and more prone to damage from frost and wind. Propagated most readily from seed sown in a soil-based compost in a cold-frame during late spring.

PROBLEMS

Scale insects and sooty mould growth.

RECOMMENDED VARIETIES

Eucalyptus is a huge genus of nearly 500 species, most too tender to be grown outdoors in Britain. The hardiest species in the herb garden is the blue gum, *E. globulus*.

Eucalyptus gunnii

Gaultheria procumbens
Wintergreen

❝ *The various species of* Gaultheria *are among a group of sound, workhorse shrubs for the ornamental garden. They are pretty enough and functional enough but they will never be stars of any border. And yet oil of wintergreen, together with witch hazel (p.116) must be among the most familiar, and probably most effective of herbal medicines still in everyday use.* ❞

HERBAL INTEREST
Culinary None.
Non-culinary An oil from the leaves has healing and pain-relievng properties and is applied to inflamed skin. An infusion is taken as a relief for sore throats.

RECOMMENDED VARIETIES
Normal species only is available.

Gaultheria procumbens

FUNCTIONAL VALUE As evergreen ground cover.

ORNAMENTAL APPEAL Small, more or less oval, glossy, dark green, evergreen leaves, bunches of drooping, white, summer flowers and bright red, autumn berries.

SITE AND SOIL Light to moderate shade in most soils, preferably acidic; intolerant of alkalinity.

HARDINESS Moderately hardy to hardy, tolerating around -15°C (5°F).

SIZE Will attain about 50 x 75cm (20 x 30in) after three years and about 50cm x 3m (20in x 10ft) eventually.

CULTIVATION AND CARE

Mulch in autumn and spring and give a balanced general fertilizer in spring. No pruning is needed but it may be cut back hard in spring and it will regenerate. Most easily propagated by removal of suckers.

PROBLEMS
None.

ILEX

Ilex aquifolium Holly

❝ *It is a curious phenomenon that everyone seems to forget about the holly plant after the festive season and then bring it to mind again for Christmas. However, there is far more to this plant than a bunch of prickly leaves and some red berries for decoration. The holly genus, Ilex, includes a very wide range of evergreen as well as many deciduous species, most without significant prickles and not all with red berries. Like box, it has long been grown for its extremely hard wood which can be worked into most attractive ornamental items but it also has unexpected and ancient herbal properties, too.* ❞

HERBAL INTEREST
Culinary None.
Non-culinary An infusion from the leaves is used to relieve congestion and colds.

CULTIVATION AND CARE
Mulch in autumn and spring and give a balanced general fertilizer in spring. The hedgehog hollies need no pruning; but others may be clipped as required in mid-summer and mid-autumn. They are all but impossible to strike from cuttings and the named forms do not come true from their seed.

PROBLEMS
Leaf miners (which are disfiguring but not damaging).

Ilex aquifolium 'Golden King'

FUNCTIONAL VALUE As either hedging or a specimen ornamental.

ORNAMENTAL APPEAL Evergreen leaves, red or yellow berries and an attractive, dense, if sometimes impenetrable habit.

SITE AND SOIL Full sun to moderate shade; tolerates most soils provided they are not extremely wet or extremely dry.

HARDINESS Very hardy, tolerating -20°C (-4°F).

SIZE Hedgehog holly will attain about 75 x 75cm (30 x 30in) after four or five years and perhaps 2 x 2m (7 x 7ft) eventually. Other varieties will attain about 1m x 50cm (3ft x 20m) after three or four years and ultimately form trees of about 10-15m (30-50ft) in height.

RECOMMENDED VARIETIES
Although there are many ornamental varieties of holly, derived from several species, it is the common holly, *Ilex aquifolium*, that has been used for herbal purposes. The best forms for the herb garden are the varieties of the dwarf, so-called hedgehog holly, 'Ferox'. 'Ferox Argentea' has silver leaf edges and 'Ferox Aurea' an irregular golden variegation. For a taller tree, choose 'J.C. Van Tol' or 'Golden Queen'.

Hamamelis virginiana Witch hazel

❝ *Witch hazel and wintergreen (p.115) are familiar names to people who haven't the remotest idea what either of the plants look like. You can walk into any pharmacy and find bottles so labelled on the shelf, as both plants produce widely used and effective soothing remedies. Witch hazel is much the more appealing of the two and is worthy of a place in any garden for its winter flowers. But it is not any easy shrub, requiring exacting conditions if it is to grow well.* ❞

HERBAL INTEREST
Culinary None.
Non-culinary An extract from the young shoots is used for the relief of bruises, inflammations and other external sores.

LAURUS

FUNCTIONAL VALUE
None.
ORNAMENTAL APPEAL
Small, fragrant, yellow flowers borne on twigs in late autumn, coincident with the foliage turning yellow before dropping. The impact, therefore, is not as great as that of the Asiatic species which flower later in the winter on bare twigs.
SITE AND SOIL
Light shade and shelter from cold winds, in moist, free-draining organic soil, ideally slightly acidic.
HARDINESS
Moderately hardy, tolerating about -15°C (5°F) but damaged by cold winds.
SIZE
Will attain 1 x 1m (3 x 3ft) after three years and up to 5-6 x 5m (15-20 x 15ft) eventually.

RECOMMENDED VARIETIES
The best known ornamental witch hazels are the Asiatic species, most notably *Hamamelis mollis*, but the best for the extraction of medicinal witch hazel is the North American *H. virginiana* which provides the rootstock on to which the ornamental forms are grafted.

CULTIVATION AND CARE
Mulch in autumn and spring and give a balanced general or rose fertilizer in spring. Do not prune. Propagation is difficult from cuttings but the true species may be raised from seed sown in pots of soil-based compost in a cold-frame; germination is slow.
PROBLEMS
None.

Laurus nobilis
Sweet bay

❝ This is perhaps the most valuable of all shrubby herbs, although I am constantly amazed by the number of people who grow it as an ornamental, generally in the form of over-priced specimens in terracotta pots, and yet still buy bay leaves from their supermarket. The number of leaves that are required in the kitchen would not make much impression on so robust a plant. ❞

HERBAL INTEREST
Culinary Leaves are used with cooked meat of all types, also with some fish and in soups and stews. Most commonly used in *bouquets garnis.*
Non-culinary A leaf infusion is used as a refreshing stimulant to the appetite.

Laurus nobilis

FUNCTIONAL VALUE
As an attractive specimen ornamental, most effective when clipped to shape.
ORNAMENTAL APPEAL
Elongated, dull green, evergreen leaves and green-yellow flowers in early summer.
SITE AND SOIL
Full sun to moderate shade with shelter from cold winds. Tolerates most soils provided not very wet, heavy and cold.
HARDINESS
Moderately hardy, tolerating -10 to -15°C (14 to 5°F) but damaged by cold winds.
SIZE
Will attain about 1.5 x 1.5m (5 x 5ft) after four or five years and, unpruned, could eventually form a tree of about 12 x 9m (40 x 28ft).

RECOMMENDED VARIETIES
The normal species is the one to choose although there is a rather more tender form, 'Aurea', supposedly golden-leaved but which to me merely looks like a sick version of the normal one.

CULTIVATION AND CARE
Mulch in autumn and spring and give a balanced general fertilizer in spring. May be clipped to shape in summer and will also regenerate from the old wood if cut back hard. Propagate from semi-ripe cuttings in a soil-based compost in a cold-frame during the summer.
PROBLEMS
Scale insects, leading to the development of sooty moulds.

MORUS

Morus nigra Black mulberry

❝ *I hesitated slightly before including mulberry as a herb plant for it really crosses my own defined boundary into being one of those plants that is grown for an edible product rather than a flavouring. But it is used for medicinal as well as straightforward edible purposes; and it is such a splendid plant that I am inclined to take whatever opportunity is open to me to urge more people to grow it.* ❞

Morus nigra

HERBAL INTEREST
Culinary Fruit eaten fresh is delicious but also good in fruit pies, jams or made into wine.
Non-culinary Fruit is used to make a laxative syrup and leaf infusion can be used by diabetics.

FUNCTIONAL VALUE
None.
ORNAMENTAL APPEAL
Deciduous and rather dull when with its greenish catkins but most attractive when covered with the dark red, raspberry-like fruit – which are notorious for dropping off the tree and staining clothing.
SITE AND SOIL Full sun in sheltered site, on rich, moist but well-drained loams.
HARDINESS Very hardy, tolerating -20°C (-4°F).
SIZE Will attain about 2 x 1m (7 x 3ft) after three or four years and become a tree up to 12m (40ft) tall eventually.

RECOMMENDED VARIETIES
The normal species is widely available although one or two named forms are also sometimes offered. The white mulberry, *Morus alba*, is a similar species to the normal one, but it has rather tasteless fruit. This is the species whose leaves are used for feeding silkworms and thus contribute to the making of silk.

CULTIVATION AND CARE
Mulch in autumn and spring and give a balanced general fertilizer in spring. No pruning is necessary. Propagate by seed sown fresh into an acidic, soilless compost or by semi-hardwood cuttings in a soil-based compost in cold-frame during summer.
PROBLEMS
None.

Myrica gale Bog myrtle

❝ *There aren't many garden shrubs that can really be called bog plants. Likewise, there aren't many herbs that thrive in really wet conditions. All of these attributes come together in this rather attractive native plant, of which I have been fond ever since I first found it growing wild with the evening sun filtering through its brown catkins. Not all herb gardens will have a suitable place for it, but a bog garden close by would be very appropriate.* ❞

HERBAL INTEREST
Culinary Leaves, after drying, are used with cooked meats, in soups and stews and also to flavour alcoholic drinks.
Non-culinary An infusion from the leaves is used to relieve gastric complaints.

CULTIVATION AND CARE
Mulch in autumn and spring and give a balanced general fertilizer in spring, at least until well established. No pruning is needed other than the cutting out of damaged branches on old trees. It may be propagated by means of the layering method if low branches are available or by hardwood cuttings in late autumn.
PROBLEMS
Fungal leaf spots and canker (a form specific to mulberries).

RECOMMENDED VARIETIES
Normal species only is available.

POPULUS

FUNCTIONAL VALUE As a bog garden ornamental.
ORNAMENTAL APPEAL Deciduous with narrowly elongated, slightly toothed and woolly leaves, brown catkins and small, greenish-yellow flowers in spring.
SITE AND SOIL Light to moderate shade, in wet, cool, acidic and also preferably organic soils.
HARDINESS Very hardy, tolerating -20°C (-4°F).
SIZE Will attain about 1 x 1m (3 x 3ft) after three or four years and up to about 2 x 2m (7 x 7ft) eventually.

Myrica gale

Populus balsamifera Balsam poplar

" *There's no denying that the balsam poplar is a really big tree and not one likely to be planted solely for its herbal appeal. Indeed, its suckering habit can create problems but the fact remains that many gardens do contain specimens planted in the past and I feel its herbal properties are interesting enough to justify my including it. The buds of the potentially giant-like tree are covered with a yellow gum, but it is the unfolding white leaves which give off the distinctive smell of balsam.* "

HERBAL INTEREST
Culinary None.
Non-culinary A fragrant oil occurs in, of all places, the leaf buds which are highly sticky and give the entire plant a characteristic aroma. When extracted, it is used for many medicinal purposes including cough remedies, lung, gastric and renal complaints, and as the basis of an antiseptic and healing ointment.

FUNCTIONAL VALUE As a screening or shelter-belt tree.
ORNAMENTAL APPEAL Deciduous with large, more or less heart-shaped, dark green leaves with whitish undersides and yellowish, pendent catkins in spring.
SITE AND SOIL Full sun, tolerates most soils provided deep, rich and fairly moist.
HARDINESS Very hardy, tolerating -20°C (-4°F).
SIZE A very vigorous plant which will attain about 2.5 x 1m (8 x 3ft) after two or three years and eventually become a tree up to 30m (100ft) tall.

Populus balsamifera

CULTIVATION AND CARE
None needed once established but damaged branches should be cut out regularly. Propagate by hardwood cuttings in autumn.
PROBLEMS
Canker, leaf curl, leaf rust, virus.

RECOMMENDED VARIETIES
Normal species only is available.

PRUNUS

Prunus dulcis Almond

❝ *Almonds can't be grown in many temperate gardens as they are rather too tender; and in most areas, they suffer frightfully from leaf curl disease. But in places where it does thrive, the almond is a most charming tree and an ideal specimen to plant close to a herb garden. The combination of spring blossom and then a crop of nuts that offer a wide range of kitchen and herbal applications is unmatched by any other tree.* ❞

HERBAL INTEREST
Culinary Nuts are used in confectionery and also with cooked fish and other savoury dishes.
Non-culinary Oil extracted from nuts is used as the basis of skin soothing and healing preparations and for minor medicinal applications.

CULTIVATION AND CARE
Mulch in autumn and spring and give a balanced general fertilizer in the spring, at least until well established. No pruning is needed other than the cutting out of damaged branches on old trees which must be done in spring or early summer to avoid the danger of infection by the fungus causing silver leaf disease. Almonds can be propagated from seed and will generally produce worthwhile plants. Commercially, they are always grafted or budded.

PROBLEMS
Peach leaf curl, silver leaf, aphids, brown rot.

FUNCTIONAL VALUE
None.

ORNAMENTAL APPEAL
Deciduous, with elongated, pointed and toothed leaves with some autumn colour. Very pretty pink or white spring blossom.

SITE AND SOIL Full sun in very sheltered and dry positions, on rich, moist but well-drained and preferably alkaline loams. In damp areas or situations, peach leaf curl disease will make almond growing impossible.

HARDINESS Moderately hardy, tolerating about -10 to -15°C (14 to 5°F) but blossom will be damaged by late frosts.

SIZE Will attain about 3 x 1m (10 x 3ft) after three or four years and become a tree up to 8-9m (25-28ft) tall eventually.

RECOMMENDED VARIETIES
Many selected varieties are fine blossom trees but of little value for almond nut production, for which you need one of the selected culinary forms but, even so, it's important to be selective for the varieties fall into two groups. Sweet almonds, generally with pink blossom, produce sweet edible nuts; bitter almonds, generally with white blossom, produce bitter nuts with poisonous kernels used for medicinal purposes. However, few varieties are available in Britain because of leaf curl disease

Prunus dulcis

Quercus spp. Oak

❝ *No-one will consider planting an oak tree simply because of its herbal value; indeed I would warn against planting oak trees in most gardens because of their potential ultimate size. But the fact remains that many large and older gardens already contain oaks, often protected by tree preservation legislation, and yet relatively few of their owners appreciate their herbal importance.* ❞

HERBAL INTEREST
Culinary Acorns can be roasted and ground to produce a coffee-like drink which was much used during the Second World War when real coffee was unobtainable.
Non-culinary Bark extracts are used to prepare various medicinal treatments, principally for blood-related problems.

ROSA

FUNCTIONAL VALUE
Provides shade and shelter.

ORNAMENTAL APPEAL
Deciduous, with indented leaves, greenish flowers in spring on mature trees, followed by acorns. Fairly good, if brief autumn colour in some years.

SITE AND SOIL
Full sun or light shade; tolerates most soils but best on rich, deep, well-drained loams.

HARDINESS
Very hardy, tolerating -20°C (-4°F).

SIZE
2 x 1m (7 x 3ft) after three or four years and eventually reaches up to 25m (80ft).

RECOMMENDED VARIETIES
There are two native oaks, *Quercus robur*, the pedunculate oak and *Q. petraea*, the sessile oak. Most existing garden trees will be of one of these species but for anyone who has space, one of the ornamental forms would be a wise choice; *Q. robur* 'Concordia', golden leaves, *fastigiata*, erect habit and 'Filicifolia', deeply divided leaves.

CULTIVATION AND CARE
Mulch in autumn and spring and give a balanced general fertilizer in spring. No pruning is needed other than the cutting out of damaged branches on old trees. Propagation from acorns, although selected forms are unlikely to come true and must be grafted; very difficult from cuttings.

PROBLEMS
Mildew, many minor leaf and branch-attacking fungi and insects often cause concern but do no harm.

Rosa spp Rose

❝ *Although the rose is no longer quite the dominant force that once it was in the English garden, it remains an extremely popular flower; and this is also true in other parts of the world. Most gardens contain at least one rose and yet I am sure not one gardener in 10,000 grows them solely for their herbal value. I certainly don't, for roses are among my most important ornamental shrubs but I do have some favourites in my herb garden.* ❞

Rosa canina

CULTIVATION AND CARE
Mulch in autumn and spring and give a balanced rose fertilizer in spring. The varieties recommended require little pruning other than the cutting out of damaged or congested shoots in spring and the removal of one or two of the oldest shoots each year. May be propagated from hardwood cuttings placed in a sheltered position in the garden in late autumn.

HERBAL INTEREST
Culinary Petals (especially of the fragrant varieties) are used in confectionery, crystallized as a garnish or to make refreshing rose water. Hips (fruit) to produce jams, syrup, wine or herbal tea, rich in vitamin C.
Non-culinary Infusion of leaves as a general 'healthy' tonic.

FUNCTIONAL VALUE
As an ornamental sheltering screen.

ORNAMENTAL APPEAL
It's worth remembering that some varieties will flower once only, some twice and some repeatedly; some have beautiful (and useful) hips; some have attractive autumn colours; and, in sheltered positions, most are more or less evergreen.

SITE AND SOIL
Full sun, ideally in a sheltered spot. Tolerate most soils except very dry ones but it always best does best in fairly heavy, moisture-retentive loams.

RECOMMENDED VARIETIES
For herbal purposes, I find invaluable *Rosa* x *alba* ('White Rose of York'), single, white; *R. canina* (dog rose), single white or pink; *R.* x *centifolia* (Provence rose), double pink; *R.* x *damascena* 'Quatre Saisons', double, loose, pink; *R. eglanteria* (sweet briar), single, pink; *R. gallica*, single, rich pink; 'Rosa Mundi', pink and white striped.

PROBLEMS
Mildew, black spot, rust, aphids.

RUBUS

Rubus fruticosus Bramble

Call it a bramble and most gardeners will spend considerable time, effort and money in trying to be rid of it. But call it a blackberry and they will carefully train and nurture it for the pleasure of picking fresh and succulent fruits in the autumn. In reality, although the best-flavoured fruits do come from wild plants, it is such a variable species that quality cannot be guaranteed and while one plant may yield a crop both delicious and bounteous, another will bear only a few shrivelled and tasteless berries. So while there is herbal value in the leaves, it makes sense to choose a selected, cultivated, fruiting variety.

HERBAL INTEREST
Culinary In addition to the obvious uses of blackberries, fresh, cooked and preserved, remember their high vitamin C content.
Non-culinary A leaf extract is used in preparations for general skin care and also in gargles and breath fresheners.

CULTIVATION AND CARE
Mulch in autumn and spring and give a balanced general fertilizer in spring. Cut out old fruited stems after the crop has been picked and tie in new shoots to training wires. Do not attempt to propagate from existing plants but buy new, virus-free stock.
PROBLEMS
Raspberry beetle, botrytis, rust, fungal leaf and cane spots.

FUNCTIONAL VALUE
When trained against a trellis or horizontal wires, may be used to form a boundary and wind-break.
ORNAMENTAL APPEAL
Deciduous (although more or less evergreen in many areas) with single white or pink flowers in spring followed by familiar fruits in late summer. Some varieties (see right) are thornless.
SITE AND SOIL
Full sun or light shade; tolerates most soils but will always crop best on rich, deep, well-drained loams, and in very dry or wet situations, will produce small, tasteless fruit.
HARDINESS
Very hardy, tolerating -20°C (-4°F).
SIZE
Varies with variety, but with correct pruning, a single plant should attain a height and spread of about 2m (7ft) within two years.

Rubus fruticosus

RECOMMENDED VARIETIES
Given that you should select a cultivated form, it is important to choose one that is not too vigorous and can readily be contained in an average-sized garden. Among several candidates, I particularly commend 'Ashton Cross' and the thornless 'Loch Ness' but I've described a wider range, with more comprehensive cultivation information in Book 4 of the series, *Best Soft Fruit*.

Taxus baccata Yew

I hope that the inclusion of yew in a book on herbs won't create the wrong impression for this is a most poisonous plant, the only non-toxic part being the red fleshy covering to the seed. But, like many another poisonous species, it does have herbal interest and as yew is also without peer as a hedging plant, there is no better boundary subject.

HERBAL INTEREST
Culinary None.
Non-culinary Various medicinal herbal remedies are prepared from foliage and fruits.

RECOMMENDED VARIETIES
For hedging, the normal species is the best plant, but for isolated specimens, choose 'Fastigiata Aurea' or 'Standishii' (both with golden foliage, columnar).

VITEX

FUNCTIONAL VALUE As a superb boundary hedge.

ORNAMENTAL APPEAL Rich, dark green foliage (or golden in selected forms) which contrasts with bright red fruits, although these will not develop on closely clipped hedges.

SITE AND SOIL Full sun to moderate shade; tolerates most soils but never successful on very dry sites.

HARDINESS Very hardy, tolerating -20°C (-4°F).

SIZE When carefully clipped, forms a hedge of 2m x 45cm (7ft x 18in) within ten years. The golden-foliaged forms will grow slowly to 2m x 45cm (7ft x 18in).

Taxus baccata

CULTIVATION AND CARE

Mulch in autumn and spring and give a general fertilizer in spring. Clip as necessary; hedges are best cut twice a year, once around mid-summer and once in mid-autumn. Propagate from seed sown in a soil-based compost in a cold-frame or from hardwood cuttings struck in a cold-frame in winter.

PROBLEMS

None.

Vitex agnus-castus Monk's Pepper

" *A plant called monk's pepper certainly sounds like a herb and yet this is one of the least familiar of all herb plants and one of the least familiar garden trees. It has pretty, late summer flowers and beautifully fragrant foliage, and the reason for its scarcity is, I'm sure, its relative tenderness, although there are many more tender and more common species. I hope that by including it and drawing attention to its virtues, I can encourage more gardeners to give it a try.* "

FUNCTIONAL VALUE None.

ORNAMENTAL APPEAL Deciduous, with large, divided fragrant leaves and slender spikes of pale blue flowers in late summer; rather reminiscent of those of *Perovskia*.

SITE AND SOIL Full sun with shelter from cold winds; ideally close to a warm wall on light, free-draining, preferably acidic soil; soils based on acidic sandstones are excellent.

HARDINESS Moderately hardy, tolerating approximately -10°C (14°F).

SIZE Will attain about 1.5 x 1m after (5 x 3ft) four or five years and about 4-5m x 2m (13-15 x 7ft) eventually.

HERBAL INTEREST

Culinary Ground seeds used as a spicy pepper substitute (although supposedly aphrodisiac too).

Non-culinary A medicinal treatment for menopausal problems is produced from the fruits.

Vitex agnus-castus

CULTIVATION AND CARE

Mulch in the autumn and the spring and give a balanced general or rose fertilizer in the spring. Do not prune. Propagate from seed sown fresh in a soil-based compost in a cold-frame or from semi-ripe cuttings in a cold-frame in the summer.

PROBLEMS

None.

RECOMMENDED VARIETIES

The normal species will be the one most likely to be seen, although there is a selected flower colour form which is called 'Blue Spire'.

INDEX

INDEX

PHOTOGRAPHIC ACKNOWLEDGEMENTS

Front cover: Clive Nichols **Back cover (inset):** Professor Stefan Buczacki

Inside photographs:

Baker Straw Partnership 47 right; Pat Brindley 57 right; Dr Stefan Buczacki 23 centre, 23 right, 23 left, 72; Eric Crichton 1, 8, 9, 33 bottom, 35 centre, 41 left, 44, 45 top, 47 left, 49, 62, 63 top, 66, 69 right, 71 right, 77 bottom left, 78 right, 87, 90 top, 92, 94 top, 97 top left, 98, 99 right, 100, 104 top, 111 bottom, 117, 122, 123 left; John Fielding 26, 31 left, 34, 39 left, 40 bottom, 40 top, 51 left, 54, 58, 60, 61 top, 79, 81 left, 91, 96, 101 top, 106 top, 118, 120; Garden Picture Library /Brian Carter 95 bottom, /Bob Challinor 102, /John Glover 97 bottom left; Garden Matters 51 right; John Glover 7, 10, 11 bottom, 18 left, 19 left, 29 top, 42, 48, 63 bottom, 69 left, 77 top, 78 left, 85, 93 left, 94 bottom, 113 left, 113 right; Jerry Harpur 88 centre, 105; Horticultural Research Institute 21 left, 21 right; Jacqui Hurst 80; Andrew Lawson 6, 11 top, 27 right, 31 centre, 32 top, 33 top, 38, 43, 53 left, 55 left, 55 right, 59 left, 67 right, 70, 75 right, 76, 77 bottom right, 84 bottom, 90 bottom, 104 bottom, 106 bottom, 108 right; Natural Image /Bob Gibbons 29 bottom, 46, 82; Nature Photographers Ltd /Andrew Cleave 53 right, /Geoff du Feu 59 centre, /Christopher Grey-Wilson 41 top right, /Jean Hall 27 left, /Paul Sterry 45 bottom, 56, 65 left, 119 left; Clive Nichols 18 top right, 19 bottom right, 19 top right, 68 top, 75 left, 89, 111 top; Oxford Scientific Films /Gordon Maclean 101 bottom; Photos Horticultural 12, 13, 14, 15, 16, 18 bottom right, 20, 28, 32 bottom, 35 left, 36, 37 left, 37 right, 50, 52, 57 left, 65 right, 68 bottom, 81 right, 83, 84 top, 86, 88 left, 103 left, 103 right, 107, 108 left, 114, 115 right, 116, 121, 123 right; Photo/Nats 64; Reed International Books Ltd /George Wright 115 left
Harry Smith Collection 17, 30, 39 right, 41 bottom right, 61 bottom, 67 left, 71 left, 73 bottom, 73 left, 74, 93 right, 95 top, 97 right, 99 left, 109, 110, 112, 119 right.

TEMPERATURE CHART

BARELY HARDY	0 to -5°C	32 to 23°F
FAIRLY HARDY	-5 to -10°C	23 to 14°F
MODERATELY HARDY	-10 to -15°C	14 to 5°F
HARDY	-15 to -20°C	5 to -4°F
VERY HARDY	-20°C or below	-4°F or below

STEFAN BUCZACKI "BEST" SERIES J502D60C

The complete range is available from all good bookshops or by Mail Order direct from the publisher. Payment can be made by credit card or cheque/postal order in the following ways:

BY PHONE Phone through your order on our special CREDIT CARD HOTLINE on **0933 410511**. Speak to our customer service team during office hours (9am to 5pm) or leave a message on the answer machine, quoting your full credit card number plus expiry date and your full name and address. Please also quote the reference number shown at the top of this form.

BY POST Simply fill out the order form below (it can be photocopied) and send it with your payment to:
REED BOOK SERVICES LTD, PO BOX 5, RUSHDEN, NORTHANTS NN10 6YX.

SPECIAL OFFER: FREE POSTAGE AND PACKAGING FOR ALL ORDERS OVER £10, add £2.00 for p+p if your order is for £10 or less.

ISBN	TITLE	PRICE	QUANTITY	TOTAL
0 600 57732 5	Best Climbers	4.99		
0 600 57735 X	Best Foliage Shrubs	4.99		
0 600 57734 1	Best Shade Plants	4.99		
0 600 57733 3	Best Soft Fruit	4.99		
0 600 58337 6	Best Water Plants	4.99		
0 600 58338 4	Best Herbs	4.99		
		Postage & Packaging (add £2 for p+p if your order is £10 or less)		
		GRAND TOTAL		

Name .... (BLOCK CAPITALS)
Address ....

.... Postcode ....

I enclose a cheque/postal order for £ .... made payable to Reed Book Services Ltd or

Please debit my: Access ☐ Visa ☐ AmEx account ☐ Diners ☐ by £ .... Expiry date ....

Account no ☐☐☐☐☐☐☐☐☐☐☐☐☐☐☐☐ Signature ....